TOSCANINI'S
FUMBLE

BANTAM NEW AGE BOOKS

This important imprint includes books in a variety of fields and disciplines and deals with the search for meaning, growth and change.

Ask your bookseller for the books you have missed.

TOSCANINI'S FUMBLE

And Other Tales of Clinical Neurology

HAROLD L. KLAWANS, M.D.

BANTAM BOOKS
NEW YORK • TORONTO • LONDON • SYDNEY • AUCKLAND

This edition contains the complete text
of the original hardcover edition.
NOT ONE WORD HAS BEEN OMITTED.

TOSCANINI'S FUMBLE AND OTHER TALES
OF CLINICAL NEUROLOGY
*A Bantam Book / published by arrangement with
Contemporary Books, Inc.*

PRINTING HISTORY
Contemporary Books edition published May 1988
Bantam edition / May 1989

Bantam New Age *and the accompanying figure design as well as
the statement "the search for meaning, growth and change" are
trademarks of Bantam Books, a division of Bantam Doubleday Dell
Publishing Group, Inc.*

Library of Congress Cataloging-in-Publication Data

Klawans, Harold L.
  Toscanini's fumble.

  1. Neurology—Anecdotes. I. Title.
[RC351.K57 1989]   616.8   88-8109
  ISBN 0-553-34662-8 (pbk.)

Published simultaneously in the United States and Canada

───────────────────────────────

*Bantam Books are published by Bantam Books, a division of Bantam
Doubleday Dell Publishing Group, Inc. Its trademark, consisting of the
words "Bantam Books" and the portrayal of a rooster, is Registered in
U.S. Patent and Trademark Office and in other countries. Marca
Registrada. Bantam Books, 666 Fifth Avenue, New York, New York 10103.*

───────────────────────────────

PRINTED IN THE UNITED STATES OF AMERICA

CWO   0 9 8 7 6 5 4 3 2 1

Contents

In Memory of My Parents

TOSCANINI'S FUMBLE

1

Prologue: Wanting to Be a Doctor, Part I

Meeting a friend in a corridor, Wittgenstein said: 'Tell me, why do people always say it was natural for men to assume that the sun went around the earth rather than that the earth was rotating?' His friend said, 'Well, obviously it just looks as if the sun is going around the earth.' To which the philosopher replied, 'Well, what would it have looked like if it had looked as if the earth was rotating?'
—Tom Stoppard, *Jumpers*, 1972

My father was a physician—an otolaryngologist, or ear, nose, and throat specialist. My father's younger brother was also a physician—an obstetrician-gynecologist. They were the two adult males I most loved and admired as I was growing up, notwithstanding Luke Appling and Nellie Fox, two heroes from my beloved White Sox. Since it was abundantly clear that I was far too slow to play major league baseball, it was only natural that I too wanted to become a physician. In an earlier age it would have been very easy to follow in my father's footsteps. Such a decision would have required absolutely no introspection on my part. As I grew older I would have become apprenticed to either my father or my uncle and then would have spent a year or so taking some courses at one medical school or other—which one wouldn't have really mattered much. And my admission to whatever school I had picked would have depended only on my interest and my father's ability to pay the fees.

Those were the days before admission committees. Today it is not so simple. You cannot become a physician by studying as an apprentice. You must attend a real medical school, and admission to any medical school is very competitive. Medical schools pick only the best students. Not the best possible physicians—no one knows how to do that—but the best students. The choice is based on grade point averages, standardized tests, letters of recommendation, and the like. But the admission committees also require an essay, which allows them to give lip service to the notion that they are choosing the best future physicians.

There I was in my third year of undergraduate work at the University of Michigan faced with the task of writing an autobiographical essay entitled "Why I Want to Be a Doctor." I felt as if I were back in fourth grade and writing about what I did on my summer vacation.

I drove home for the weekend to discuss it with my dad. Why had he gone into medicine? His father had not been a physician. He had owned a tavern, and later, during Prohibition, he had sold insurance. My father had not followed in his father's footsteps, so why was I following my father's footsteps? Was it merely to follow in his footsteps? What would I have done had he been an insurance man or a tavern owner? What did I know about being a physician? What did any twenty-year-old undergraduate know? My dad and I spent the weekend talking together. Or rather he talked and I listened. He talked about what it meant to him to be a physician, about how medicine combined science and the humanities and about the "art of medicine." He focused particularly on the way in which a physician influences the lives of his patients and how the patients, their problems, and their ways of coming to terms with their problems in turn influence the physician's life.

Sunday after dinner I drove back to Ann Arbor, and on Monday I wrote my essay. It contained the usual sophomoric regurgitation of all the ideas I had heard over the weekend and had somehow transformed into clichés. On Tuesday I sent out my completed applications, and for the next eight years I gave no further thought to that conversation or the entire subject of why I had wanted to be a physician. I was too busy learning to be a doctor and answering another question: what type of doctor would I become?

This answer came easily and logically. I did not want to be any kind of surgeon at all. My hands, like my legs, were too slow. That meant that, despite the wishes of my role models, I would be neither an otolaryngologist nor an obstetrician-gynecologist.

What fascinated me was the brain. How did the left side of the brain control the right side of the body? And why? It was not just the road maps of the anatomy of the nervous system that intrigued me, but also the quasiphilosophical issues of the origin and organization of speech, and especially the problem-solving nature of neurology. So I became a neurologist.

This book is a product of those same interests. It is about the brain and, to a far lesser extent, the rest of the nervous system. Mostly it's about what happens when something goes wrong inside the brain and how that brain, or at least one part of that brain, can no longer do whatever it is it usually does so efficiently. The affected person is no longer a normal person. He has been transformed into a patient, a patient with a neurological deficit. Figuring out where that area of dysfunction is located within that brain is the puzzle-solving detective work of neurology. Discovering why dysfunction in that area causes whatever alteration in function the patient manifests is more than a philosophical problem; it is the core to our understanding the brain. It is the science of *neurology* and gives birth to the various areas of research I have pursued for almost two decades of my life.

Unfortunately, that is what we understand best about the brain—not the normal function of the brain and its parts, but the way in which these functions are altered by disease or destruction of one part or another. For example, a small group of neurons (nerve cells) are called the *substantia nigra*, or black substance, because they contain the black pigment known as melanin. Each of us has two such nuclei or collections of neurons, one on each side of our brain stem. The Ancients knew all about this structure and in fact named it, but they had no idea what it did. About the turn of the century, all of that changed. Pathologists and neurologists discovered that patients with Parkinson's disease had lost the pigmented cells of their substantia nigra. The scientists concluded that Parkinson's disease is related to destruction of this structure.

What is the function—the precise function—of the substantia nigra within the intact, uninjured brain? I have been asking that question for twenty years. To date the best answer seems to be to prevent Parkinson's disease.

In a way this is no more than a refocusing of an age-old issue. How does whatever happens inside the brain become behavior? What is the neurochemical basis of thought? The neuroanatomical basis of memory? Each year, each month, we learn more about the basic chemical and anatomical facts of our brain. Yet it is unclear whether we are getting any closer to translating these basic processes into complex human behaviors such as speech and memory.

Brain cells are really quite simple. These neurons have lost many of the properties shared by other cells. Once formed, they cannot reproduce themselves. They merely specialize in receiving, generating, and transporting messages. Each nerve cell is covered with receptors. Other nerve cells release chemicals onto these receptors. Some chemicals stimulate the receptors, while others inhibit them. If enough receptors are stimulated, the neuron fires and sends an electrical message to its own terminals, where that electrical impulse releases its chemicals onto the receptors of other neurons. That in essence is the entire story. Somehow everything we do derives from that process.

I do not know precisely what happens when each transmitter hits its specific receptors; I don't think that anyone really does. I certainly don't know how transmitter-receptor interactions translate into complex functions. Yet I know that many diseases result from alterations in specific neurotransmitter-neuroreceptor relationships. These diseases include Parkinson's disease, Huntington's chorea, and perhaps even schizophrenia, or at least drug-induced schizophrenic reactions. I have included a number of these problems in this collection, in the hope of giving you some insight into these disorders and what they teach us about the brain.

It was the ancient Greeks who first made the brain-behavior issue into a philosophical conundrum. It was likewise the Ancients who realized that one side of the brain controls the movements of the opposite side of the body. Knowing and reading the maps of the nervous system is the art of neurological diagnosis. The neurologist collects each patient's signs and symptoms, and if he knows all the charts, which are what he has been trained to know, he can figure out precisely where the problem is. It's a form of puzzle solving, no different from many other such exercises. I have included some clinical examples of these issues, which are what I teach neurology residents. Each of them explains very little about what makes us what we are.

Problem solving and research were not all that made neurology so attractive to me as a student. It was the role of the neurologist as problem solver, not as healer of the ill or friend of the sick. An old story about the various neurological specialties has been told in medical circles since the time my father was in medical school: The neurologist knows much and does little. The neurosurgeon knows little and does much. The neuropathologist knows everything one day too late for anyone to do anything.

I was so young and naive that I thought my father was wrong—medicine was science and learning and research, not patients and their broken lives in need of help and repair. Then I finished my training, and the neurological problems I had learned to diagram so well became my patients. Their lives began to shape my life; their problems slowly became my problems.

No physician can be all things to all patients. Each physician tries to be as much of a humanist as he can, but the physician and the patient both demand that he never depart from his role as scientist. Balancing the two is difficult. Juggling a third role, that of teacher, adds another complication. If I err in balancing these three demands, I undoubtedly err in the direction of teacher. A good friend once described me as a "compulsive teacher." It is a charge of which I am guilty. In at least one sense, this book is of course part of that compulsive trait.

I have published two novels. I wrote the first, *Sins of Commission*, because I wanted to write a book that would explain how the skill of the neurological diagnosis can be taught. In a more limited sense, this book addresses the same issue.

This book is not a novel; however, neither is it a series of unrelated scientific papers, each entirely self-contained and self-sufficient. It is a series of essays that should be entertaining as well as educational and is aimed not at the specialist but at the general reader. For this reader, the book explains various terms, theories, concepts, and anatomical structures in some detail. Yet to explain them each time they appear would be far too repetitious. So, while most of the contributions can stand alone, the book is designed to be read from front to back.

As I have been working on this introduction, I have realized that it was at least in part my need to learn that drove me first into medicine and neurology and finally into the type of neurological career I have pursued. That need and the need to teach have become one and the same. I need to understand, and I want others also to understand. So I do research and I teach and I write and I care for patients, for it is in caring for them that I learn the most about what the brain can and can't do and how we as individuals can cope despite these limitations.

The opening anecdote about Wittgenstein probably applies as well to our knowledge of the brain as it does to our understanding of the solar system. We accept many notions because they seem to be the logical answers to our questions. But have we asked the right questions?

The tremor that so distresses patients with Parkinson's disease invariably goes away during sleep, only to return the next morning as soon as the patient awakens. This is a fact, a clinical observation that has been documented thousands and thousands of time. Yet no one knows why this occurs. Each medical student learns this fact when he studies neurology. The inquisitive student recognizes the strangeness of this and asks, "Why does the tremor go away during sleep?" That is not the real issue. During sleep the brain is functioning normally and producing normal behavior. The real problem is to understand why the tremor comes back the next morning.

We, like Wittgenstein, must be smart enough to ask the right question. That is the hardest part of being a scientist.

2
"Did I Remove That Gallbladder?"

Ken Keltner's* name is not a household word. It never has been and never will be. After all, the names of only a select number of surgeons ever fall into that category, and most of them are cardiovascular surgeons: DeBakey, Christian Barnard. Ken Keltner is a general surgeon; gallbladders, hemorrhoids, and hernias are his turf—with varicose veins for variety—not coronary artery bypasses or heart transplants or valve replacements. Nothing that glamorous.

By the time he came to see me as a patient in 1986, we'd known each other professionally for over twenty years. We were not friends but professional colleagues who respected each other and had shared patients off and on for two decades. Ken is well respected as a general surgeon. He doesn't teach or do any research. He doesn't even have a faculty appointment at any of Chicago's six medical schools. But he does general surgery better than most surgeons, including those with appointments at the various medical schools. In his own part of

---

*All names have been changed for the purpose of this book.

the world, the far western suburbs of Chicago, he's considered a doctor's doctor, one of those rare individuals other doctors trust to operate on them and members of their own families.

Ken arrived at my office at five minutes to eleven, accompanied by a nurse named Joan Gordon. Both were still garbed in their green surgical scrub suits. Ken looked tired. His face, which often appeared boyish for a man in his middle fifties, now clearly showed his age. He walked with his usual rapid, confident stride, but something was different. Normally when Ken Keltner walked into a room, everyone felt his presence, his strength of personality. But this time it was almost as if no one had entered my office.

I greeted him by name as one colleague to another, and he in turn greeted me by name. I was glad that he could do that much. I'd been prepared for the worst. When Joan called, she'd told me that Ken had had a stroke and was completely delirious.

Before I had a chance to say anything more, he asked two questions. He asked them in rapid succession without waiting for any reply in between. "Where am I? What's happening to me?"

His voice was flat. It betrayed no emotion at all—no fear, no concern, no bewilderment. Nor did his eyes. Nor his face. The most I could sense was a mild degree of curiosity, not a driving interest—far from it. It was more like a totally detached curiosity as if he were pursuing some minor academic point about gallbladder surgery, something he probably ought to know but nothing that would affect his life or alter his behavior.

He repeated his two questions once again: "Where am I? What's happening to me?"

Once again he didn't pause in between for a reply. And for the second time, it seemed that the process of asking was more important to him than any answers his questions might evoke.

"You are in my office, Ken," I replied. "I'm going to examine you."

He nodded as if he understood what I said to him.

I paused.

He asked his two questions once again: "Where am I? What's happening to me?"

My answer had not gotten through. He might have understood it briefly, but that understanding had not been incorporated into his consciousness.

"Where am I? What's happening to me?"

Once again I answered his questions and watched him nod in return. Before he got a chance to ask them again, I asked Joan to describe what she had observed.

The story she told me was a remarkable one. Even though she'd never received any training in neurological nursing and she didn't really understand what had happened, she was able to reconstruct what had happened in minute detail. She'd sensed right at the beginning that something was not right and had tried hard to notice and remember exactly what happened.

They'd been in the operating room for over an hour and a half. It was the same O.R. they worked in together three mornings a week, week after week, year after year. In addition to Joan, who was the scrub nurse, three people were in the O.R.: Ken Keltner, the anesthetist, and the patient, Vera Bickford. Ken was removing her gallbladder. The operation had gone smoothly and quickly. He was a quick surgeon; he made decisions rapidly, and his hands moved quickly.

Then he did something he rarely did. He looked up at the clock on the wall of the operating room. Joan looked, too. It was 9:43. They'd begun the operation at 8:05.

"One hour and thirty-eight minutes," he said. She couldn't remember the last time he'd cared how long an operation had taken. "I'll be done in another five or six minutes," he continued.

That was obvious to her. They had done hundreds of gallbladders together. All that was left to do was to suture Mrs. Bickford's abdominal wall closed.

"Skin to skin in one hour and forty-three minutes," he said.

"Not bad," she replied.

"Not bad at all," he echoed. "Especially for a fifty-eight-year-old general surgeon who works without residents."

She could not remember his ever having said anything like that. Working at a hospital without residents was his own choice. And she hadn't known that he was fifty-eight. She'd thought he was younger than that.

This was, he told her, the sixteen hundred and forty-second gallbladder he'd removed during his career as a general surgeon. At one time he'd debated putting metal tags on each gallbladder as he removed them. Metal tags with consecutive numbers. They did that with the duck at that restaurant in Paris. "What was the name of that restaurant?" he wondered out loud.

Joan had no idea. She'd never been to Paris. By now she was afraid something was wrong. Ken was normally all business during an operation, and this was not business. The operation had come to a standstill, work remained to be done.

"It's on the Left Bank," he mused. "Just beyond Notre Dame, with a great view of the back of Notre Dame."

She knew what she had to do. She handed him the forceps with the needle and suture already loaded into it. He took it just as he always had and put in the first suture. And the second. And the third. It would take a total of about nine or ten more. Then Mrs. Bickford would have a nice thin scar.

"What was the name of that restaurant?" he asked again.

"Which one?"

"The one with the numbered ducks."

"The one in . . ."

"Where was that restaurant?"

She handed him another suture, and he put it in.

"What restaurant?" he asked.

Joan had no interest at all in restaurants, in Paris or not. She wanted to know why Ken Keltner was thinking about restaurants instead of this operation. And the next one. Did he remember that he had another operation to do immediately after Mrs. Bickford? On somebody named Mitchell. She reminded him.

He looked at her blankly.

He couldn't have forgotten, thought Joan. He never forgot anything about his patients. Perhaps he hadn't understood.

"What's our next operation?" she asked as cheerfully as she could.

"A hernia," he said. "Or a vein stripping. Or something." He couldn't remember.

She looked at the half-closed wound. He had put in five sutures. That left about six more to go. And he was just standing there as if he had no idea what he should do next. He looked up at her.

The nurse smiled at him.

"Did I take out that gallbladder?" he asked.

Joan was so startled she couldn't make any reply.

"Did I take out that gallbladder?" he repeated.

"Yes," she said. "Everything went well."

"Good," he said. Then after a pause, "Did I take out that gallbladder?"

"The operation's almost over," she said. She reached over and picked up the gallbladder that had been removed about twenty minutes earlier and showed it to him. "Here's the gallbladder. You see that it's been removed."

"Yes," he nodded. Ken stood there motionless.

Joan still did not know what was wrong, but she knew that something was. And it was serious. A stroke, she thought. He must be having a stroke. "You are closing up," she said, taking complete charge of the operating room. "You have already put in about five sutures. Take the forceps and put in another one."

"Yes," he said. "Closing up. I see."

Ken began to put in the next stitch. Joan watched him critically. As far as she could tell, he did it as deftly and quickly as ever. The distance from the previous one was perfect, and so was the closure of the wound—excellent opposition of the two sides, no excess puckering. He was a meticulous surgeon. That, she told me, was why she liked working with him, why she'd been working with him for a dozen years. That was also why she'd let him take out her own gallbladder three years ago.

He was done tying the knot. He should have started the next stitch. Instead he asked the same question: "Did I take out that gallbladder?"

"Yes," she replied.

"Oh," he nodded. "What am I doing now?"

"You are closing up."

"Oh," he said with almost a touch of insight.

"Closing up," she repeated.

"Closing up," he said.

"Put in the next suture," she instructed him.

Ken went back to work. Once again Joan scrutinized his every move. If he did anything wrong, she'd have to call for help, to get someone else into the O.R. to close up. She wanted to avoid that if she possibly could, but she couldn't endanger the patient in any way.

Ken stopped. He had put in one more perfect suture, and he once again began his litany. "Did I take out that gallbladder?"

There was one difference this time. He did not wait for an answer before he asked his second question: "What am I doing?"

Slowly, carefully, and firmly, Joan answered his questions and told him what to do. Once again he followed her instructions.

The process went on. Suture. Knot. Questions: "Did I take out that gallbladder? What am I doing?" Instructions. Suture. Questions.

By the time they'd finished, he'd added a third question to his routine: "Where am I?"

Finally, he had put in the last suture. Joan had talked him through the operation. Mrs. Bickford's abdomen was closed. The scar was straight. The two sides were aligned perfectly. Ken had closed Mrs. Bickford's surgical incision as well as he had closed up any gallbladder Joan had assisted him on in the last dozen years. Technically his hands had performed their job as well as ever. Joan looked at the clock. It had taken ten minutes, about five minutes longer than it should have. It had seemed far longer than that to her. She was thankful that he'd been able to finish the operation.

That was when she had called my office and told my secretary that she was bringing Ken in to see me. She was sure that he had had a stroke—a small stroke, but nonetheless a stroke.

Ken had stood there quietly throughout Joan's entire description of what had happened to him, not interrupting her even once. This was a man who normally was impatient with long, drawn-out explanations, always anxious to get to the bottom line, but he'd said nothing. He had to have heard every word she'd said. Had he understood it all? Had he understood any of it? Did he now understand what had happened to him and what was happening to him?

His expression had not changed a bit. He still had the same detached yet mildly curious look on his face. His repertoire also remained the same: "Where am I? What's happening to me?"

Obviously, any attempt to derive further information about the present episode from him would be an exercise in futility. Facts obtained through language, the way most of us learn most of what we ever learn, were not being learned by Ken. Despite being told numerous times that he had successfully removed Mrs. Bickford's diseased gallbladder, he didn't know that he had removed it. And showing him the gallbladder hadn't helped either; the nonverbal stimulus had made no difference. So his problem was not merely a failure to understand language.

His problem was learning and memory. Ken could not learn new facts. He could not incorporate what he heard or saw or felt into his memory.

And his problem extended beyond brand new facts or experiences. He had been in my office at least a dozen times before, yet he didn't know where he was. Two days a week for the past twenty years or more, he had been operating in the same operating room in the same hospital; yet once this episode had taken hold, he didn't know where he was or what he was doing.

Memory is a complex and only partially understood activity of the brain. Neurologists often divide it into three separate components: immediate, recent, and remote. While these three functions are often defined as separate entities, they actually are not. They blend into each other, and any such divisions are arbitrary at best.

Immediate memory is the ability to recall something as soon as it has been learned or presented. This is formally tested by asking a patient to repeat a three-digit number.

Try it: 2-7-1.

Close your eyes, and repeat the number. Child's play, right?

Then four digits: 6-3-2-8. Then five. Then six. Then seven: 9-4-2-8-0-1-0. For that one, I always use my own phone number. That way I don't forget what number I've given the patient.

Next I show the patient three objects and ask him to name them—a key, a quarter, and a comb, or whatever else is in my pocket at the time. I then put the objects back in my pocket and ask the patient to name them again. So much for testing immediate memory.

"Where am I?" Ken asked for the fortieth time.

"Ken," I said forcefully, "you are in my office."

He nodded.

"Now," I asked, "where are you?"

"Where am I?"

There was no need for numbers or keys. His immediate memory was not functioning at all.

Recent memory involves the ability to recall after a time delay. The delay can be one of minutes or hours or days. Any definition of when immediate recall ends and recent memory begins is arbitrary, but most authorities agree that any recall that occurs after a delay of several minutes is a function of the process of recent memory. Recent memory requires some sort of chemical change that can persist for hours or days. Immediate recall requires no such long-lasting alteration.

How is this tested? What were those three objects I named for you and then put back in my pocket five minutes ago? A key, a quarter, and a comb. Don't feel bad if you missed one or two. I hadn't asked you to remember them.

Next I ask the patient about recent events in his life. What did you have for lunch? For dinner last night? What did you do last night?

The segment of Ken's recent memory that covered the time for which he had no immediate recall could not be functioning.

If a patient is unable to recall the names of three objects immediately, then there is no way he will be able to come up with
those names after a delay of five or ten minutes.

But his defects in recent memory were more extensive than
that. He didn't even recall starting the operation, and that had
been before this episode had begun.

Did he know what he'd had for breakfast?

He didn't.

Or what he'd done the night before?

He had absolutely no idea. Recent memory was part of the
problem.

But what about Ken's remote memory? *Remote memory*, which
is what we usually consider memory, encompasses the ability
to recall after weeks and months. The chemical process may
involve the production of new proteins within the brain; in any
case, remote memory does involve a rather persistent or permanent chemical change.

I was certain that this type of memory was at least partially
functioning. Why? Because he recalled facts that he had
learned in the past. He had recognized me. He had seen me,
known who I was, and recalled my name. His simple "Harold"
had shown that he could recall faces and names and could
connect the two. His nonverbal recall of faces worked, and so
did his memory for names.

I also knew that he had retained other types of information.
According to Joan, he had closed the incision as technically well
as ever. His technical skills had been retained, although she
had had to tell him what to do. He did not know where he was
or what he had to do; he could not see the open wound and
understand that he had to suture it shut. But the ability of his
brain to direct his hands and fingers in the appropriate way had
been preserved; each suture was perfectly placed.

He could remember faces and names and skills. The fact that
at least parts of his remote memory were preserved did not
surprise me, for certain aspects of remote memory are almost
impossible to destroy. People always remember who they are.
Ken did; he never asked, "Who am I?" (The only exceptions are
patients with severe psychiatric disorders and characters in

soap operas. My definition of a soap opera is an art form that allows a patient to develop total amnesia and yet form new memories.) And people always recognize loved ones and people they have known for years. Ken remembered people he knew; he never asked Joan who she was.

But was his remote recall completely intact? That was the next question I had to ask.

There are always two steps in making a neurological diagnosis. The first step is to define precisely the nature and extent of the neurological dysfunction. The neurologist does this by taking a careful history and then performing a neurological examination. Once this is completed, the doctor knows what is working inside the brain and what isn't. By applying his knowledge of the anatomy and physiology of the brain, he can tell where the lesion is and whether there is more than one area of abnormality. This is the key step and requires no knowledge of diseases.

Once this question is answered, the doctor can address the second question: What caused the abnormal function? Thus, the process boils down to two questions:

1. In what way is the brain not working right?
2. What is causing that malfunction?

Taking the first step—defining the way or ways in which Ken's brain was malfunctioning—involved answering two questions:

1. What were the nature and extent of his memory loss? Was it limited to learning and immediate or very recent memory, or was his memory for events that occurred long ago also affected to any measurable degree?

2. What were the nature and extent of any other neurological symptoms he might have developed?

While the first question may seem difficult to answer, it is in fact quite simple. All it requires is some general knowledge and a bit of bravado. There are events and facts that no healthy adult with a normal brain should ever forget. They vary with the experience and educational level of the individual patient, and of course the examiner does not always know the answers, but that shouldn't prevent him from asking the questions. Few patients fabricate answers. Those who do are readily given away upon careful questioning.

What questions does everyone know? Where he was born, the date, the name of the hospital, his mother's first name. As the testing goes on, the questions get more difficult: the names of his brothers and sisters, the birth order and relative ages of his siblings, his mother's maiden name. The list can go on and on, and of course can result in a virtual biography: name of grammar school, name of high school, job history, social history, names of his children, dates of their births, and so on. He should have been able to answer them all.

This approach has its limits, however. Much of this material is "overlearned," so a patient can recall these facts but still have serious gaps in his memory. Therefore, questioning the patient about less overlearned facts is often a better technique to detect less overt degrees of remote memory loss. For some reason, the classic neurological approach to this has been to ask the patient to perform tasks such as listing the names of the presidents backward starting with Reagan.

Try it—without looking at the list that follows.

Not so easy was it? I never expect a patient to list presidents before 1900. But even with that limitation, it still isn't so simple to do. The correct answer is:

Reagan
Carter
Ford (so easily forgotten)
Nixon
Johnson
Kennedy
Eisenhower
Truman
Roosevelt
Hoover
Coolidge
Harding
Wilson

Taft
Roosevelt
The problem is that lots of people never *cared* who the president was, and besides, many who did can't name them in reverse order. After all, how well did you do? And you thought you were one of those who cared.

I remember one particular patient I saw in consultation about ten years ago. The residents had asked me to see him just to make sure they had not missed anything. He was about eighty, and when admitted to the hospital with pneumonia he'd been confused. As his pneumonia had cleared, however, so had his confusion. But the house staff was very concerned about his memory loss. He couldn't list a single past president. In fact, he didn't even know who the current president was. Nor did he know the name of the current or past governors of Illinois. (Since Illinois has had a series of governors who are singularly forgettable, that may not have been a fair question.)

He *did* know the deceased mayor of Chicago, Hizzoner Mayor Daley. But everyone knew him, even patients with significant degrees of dementia. For a Chicagoan, knowing Daley's name was like knowing one's own name or place of birth. Such material is not just learned once and then stored in the brain; it is overlearned and rarely, if ever, forgotten.

Why? Overlearned facts are probably stored in multiple areas of the brain. Single strokes cannot remove all of the traces. Since the chemical changes that underlie these facts have been so reinforced over the years, few, if any, diseases can undo them.

For this patient, Mayor Daley was the only political figure who crossed the line and became overlearned. The old man could not think of the name of one other politician. Not FDR. Not JFK. Only Richard J. Daley. Hizzoner would have been proud.

The old man wasn't sure he had ever heard the name of any other mayor of Chicago. Certainly the name Michael Bilandic, then the mayor of Chicago, was unfamiliar to him. But then Bilandic, the successor to Daley, was singularly forgettable.

Giving up on politics, I started with the biographical questions. The old man got them all right. He gave brief, sharp, rapid answers. The medical students and residents were surprised.

I stopped when I learned he had had only two years of schooling, in rural Georgia. What next? His lack of formal education was a barrier to formal intellectual testing. "Are you a baseball fan?" I asked.

He was.

"Cubs or Sox?"

"Cubs."

"What happened in 1938?"

"The homer in the dark to win the pennant."

"Who hit it?"

"Gabby Hartnett," he answered. "Why, everybody knows that."

Everybody doesn't. In fact, no one else in the room did, aside from the patient and me. "Gabby died," I informed him. I guessed that he wouldn't know. The ex–Cub Hall of Fame catcher had died only ten days earlier.

He looked at me with astonishment. "When?" he asked.

"Last week."

"I didn't know."

Of course not. He'd been incommunicado inside an oxygen tent.

There was little more to test. To test his more recent memory, I asked him about the last season's Cub players, and he passed with flying colors. "Did you ever know the names of the presidents?" I asked.

"Only one."

"Grover Cleveland."

He nodded.

One of the residents remained skeptical. He was obviously not a baseball fan and certainly not a Cub fan. He wanted to know how I could be certain the patient hadn't lied to me about the facts of his own history.

I couldn't prove it, but I knew. Even the most ardent baseball fan knows his mother's name better than Gabby Hartnett's, and no disease that I ever heard of erases the former from a patient's memory before the latter. Besides, he made an association that no patient with significant memory loss or dementia could make.

"What was that?" the resident said.

"Alexander," I said.

The resident was lost.

"Grover Cleveland Alexander was a pitcher, one of the greatest ever. A Hall of Famer, like Gabby Hartnett. Alexander was named after a president, Grover Cleveland. And that was the one president the patient knew."

Unfortunately, not everyone is a baseball fanatic. There are, however, events that allow the questioner to tell whether or not a patient's memory is intact. Events that should be recalled in full detail by all normal adults.

Try answering these questions in as much detail as you can. Choose the right ones, depending upon your age: What were you doing when you heard that Kennedy (the president, not Bobby) had been shot? What do you recall about that weekend? What were you doing when you heard that Martin Luther King, Jr., was killed? What do you recall about that weekend? VJ day? VE day? Roosevelt's death (FDR, not Teddy)? Roosevelt's funeral? Pearl Harbor? Lindy's landing in Paris? Or, more recently, the first space walk? The *Challenger* disaster?

That was a lot easier than the reverse-order list of presidents, wasn't it? Such questions, therefore, are more likely to differentiate normal from abnormal.

To test the extent of Ken Keltner's memory loss, I started with Kennedy's assassination.

Ken knew precisely what he had been doing on that fateful day. He'd just finished surgery, a gallbladder followed by a double hernia repair. He left the postoperative area and went to the waiting room to talk with the relatives of his patients. The TV was on, and the relatives were huddled around it. They told him what had happened. They hardly asked him about the operations. He remembered seeing the building on

TV. The Texas School Book Depository. He remembered Oswald and Ruby. And seeing Ruby kill Oswald. So much for 1963.

He also remembered less shocking events in clear detail—the Army-McCarthy hearings, the ticker tape carrying names of each American POW crossing the thirty-eighth parallel from North Korea to freedom. His remote memory was obviously intact.

I asked him to describe a gallbladder operation, from incision to closing. He did it without hesitation. It was like listening to someone read from a textbook of surgical techniques. "When did you do your most recent gallbladder surgery?" I asked.

He wasn't sure.

"How about your most recent hernia?" I asked.

Same response.

"Appendix?"

"I did one on Christmas Eve," he said.

That was the last operation he could remember. He remembered it, and everything that had happened before it, quite well. But after that—zero. He remembered nothing.

The rest of his exam was entirely normal. There was no weakness or paralysis, no sensory loss, no incoordination, no abnormalities of his balance or gait, no speech difficulties, no difficulty identifying objects, following instructions, or spelling words either forward or backward.

I was done. I told him not to worry, he was going to make a complete recovery. He shrugged. Did he have any questions, I asked.

Yes, he did. "Where am I? What's happening to me?"

I told him, and he asked again. I knew further reassurance would not help. I stepped outside his room, counted to ten, and walked back in. I said hello.

He smiled and said hello. He recognized me and called me by name. "When did I see you last?" I asked.

"About a month or two ago. At a meeting. Don't you remember? One of the guys wasted so much time. You were far too patient with him."

I did remember—almost as well as he did. The meeting had

been about two months ago, before Christmas. Before the appendectomy he had been able to recall.

The answers to all these questions enabled me to complete the first step of neurological diagnosis—determining the nature and extent of the brain malfunction. Ken Keltner had a circumscribed defect of memory. The rest of the functions of his brain were completely normal. Defining the nature and the extent of this defect had also given me the diagnosis, for only one disorder does this.

Dr. Kenneth Keltner, general surgeon, was in the midst of an attack of one of medicine's most startling syndromes, transient global amnesia, or TGA as it is called by those who love acronyms. A little over thirty years ago, two American neurologists from Boston, C. Miller Fisher and Raymond D. Adams, coined the term *transient global amnesia* to describe self-limited episodes in which the only major alteration in behavior is a marked disruption of memory. (The French use a different term to describe the same event: *ictus amnésique*, or amnesic attack. No one uses an acronym for this; it's one of the advantages of being French.)

Episodes like this occur in middle age or later life. They start abruptly, as did Ken's; one moment the patient is normal, the next moment he isn't. Often they start after emotional or physical stress. Sometimes they don't.

Others, not the sufferer, notice TGA. The patient's behavior may change. He may become restless, bewildered, or unusually quiet. His mind may start to wander. That was what Joan Gordon had noticed first. Dr. Keltner, usually all business during an operation, had started to wonder about the time, the length of the operation, the number of gallbladders he had removed in his career, the name of a French restaurant. Then the patient begins to ask questions. The questions always have to do with the present or the immediate past. And the patient repeats the questions over and over again, no matter how many times they are answered.

The questions are usually similar: Where am I? What's wrong? What's happening to me? At times they are tied to recent events: Did I take out that gallbladder?

Aside from learning and memory, the patient is normal, as was Ken. The sufferer cannot lay down new memories and often cannot recall events of the past few hours, days, or even weeks. But he can read, write, calculate, and even perform such skilled tasks as suturing an abdomen. Although Ken could not recall that he had to close Mrs. Bickford's abdomen, when told to do so, he put in the stitches with his usual skill.

Attacks of transient global amnesia are short and self-limited. They come on unexpectedly and depart on their own—hence the term *transient*. An episode usually lasts only a few hours, rarely hanging on for a day or two. All types of learning and recall are involved. The patient cannot remember what he sees, reads, hears, smells, tastes, or feels—hence the term *global*. There is often some retrograde loss of memory, an inability to recall events that took place immediately before the attack began—hence the term *amnesia*. This usually goes back for hours and days, but sometimes can extend back far longer. The last operation Ken could recall had taken place six weeks earlier.

When the episode is over, the patient is able to function as well as he could previously, with a major exception: He has absolutely no memory for the event itself, and he may have a short additional period of retrograde amnesia for the days or hours preceding the onset. Aside from this permanent memory gap, everything is back to normal.

Once he recovers, the patient is often quite concerned, of course. He is aware that something has happened to him and left him with a blank spot in his life. The family members who witnessed what actually happened are far more frightened, often petrified. They all have the same worries, and they all ask the same questions: Was it a stroke? Is it a warning that the patient will have a stroke? Was it the beginning of epilepsy? Was it the beginning of Alzheimer's disease? Will it come back? If it does happen again, can it be permanent? Irreversible?

Mrs. Keltner arrived at my office just as I finished examining her husband. She asked me about him, and I told her what I had told him. She talked to him and then asked me the usual barrage of questions.

I tried to answer them all, but it wasn't easy. There's a lot we don't know about transient global amnesia, but we do know enough to reassure the families that none of their fears are justified. That's what I told Mrs. Keltner. Her husband had not had a stroke. This was not a warning sign. He wasn't destined to have a stroke. It wasn't the beginning of some sort of epilepsy or Alzheimer's disease. It would probably never happen again. Even if it did, it would go away again. Less than 10 percent of patients have a second episode, and it's rare to have more than two or three such attacks. No one's life has become a series of gaps due to recurrent experiences of TGA. It comes and goes, and when it goes, it's gone.

But she persisted. What had really happened to her husband?

That question was harder to answer. The fact is that we don't really know. We only have some theories. Once again I told Ken that he would recover, but it made no difference. I reassured his wife once again. I'm not sure she believed me at first—like most wives of physicians, she took whatever any physician said skeptically—but at least she did not repeat her questions. She let it go at that.

What causes an episode of TGA? For some reason, and the reason may not be the same in all patients, the areas of the brain that are critical for the registration of memory and for memory retrieval turn off only to turn on again. How could this happen? We aren't sure. The key to understanding TGA may be the fact that such episodes often are precipitated by specific events. These events include a wide variety of acute stresses, such as:

- Immersion in very cold water. An interesting example of this was at one time labeled "amnesia by the seaside." While it has usually involved saltwater, episodes have followed a swim in fresh water or even a pool.

- Sudden exposure to cold.
- Sudden immersion in a hot bath or shower.
- Physical exercise or exertion.
- Sexual intercourse.
- Sudden emotional stress. This includes a long list of activities, from receiving an obscene phone call to witnessing the death of a spouse.
- An acute painful experience such as a dental extraction.

Memory is a complex process that involves wide areas of the brain. Two of the most important areas are regions on the undersurface of the temporal lobes at the base of the brain. Destruction of one of these causes no permanent memory loss, but destruction of both causes total inability to ever lay down a new memory.

To know what can suddenly turn off memory, we would have to understand what turns it on, and we don't know that. Memory, like most mental functions, turns off when we sleep and turns back on each morning as if the same activating system that alerts consciousness switches memory back into gear. But memory doesn't always switch on simultaneously or completely. We all have had times when our memory did not turn on. We wake up in the morning, and for a few moments we don't know where we are or what we're supposed to do. Then it clicks in; we remember. This also happens at other times, often when we're drowsy and suddenly need to function alertly. The mind is a blank; including the memory. Then all of a sudden everything switches back on. The switching on of memory every morning when we wake up is so automatic that we take it for granted, like a car shifting gears by itself.

Sometimes, however, the switch fails. Often this failure is caused by some acute, unusual stress. How? Why? I have no idea. It's as if our gears become worn with age and less reliable, so that a sudden shock can shift us from one gear to another temporarily, until our gears fall back into place.

The analogy, while crude, isn't totally inappropriate. Deep within the substance of the brain is a network of cells called the *reticular activating system*. One of the functions of this system is to maintain consciousness. It also supplies a necessary input that drives many of the brain's functions. One of these is consciousness itself, another is attention, and a third is learning and memory. The reticular system, when active or "switched on," supplies drive to the rest of the brain.

So that's what happened to Ken. The drive for learning and memory got switched off. The parts of his brain that underlie memory were left intact, so his remote memory was normal.

Ken was admitted to the hospital, and over the next six hours his memory recovered completely except for a gap of some forty-eight hours. We did all the right tests (more to reassure the patient and his wife than for any other reason): CT scan, NMR scan, EEG. The results were all normal. The next day we discharged Ken. Within two days he was back at work in the OR.

I still see him about once or twice a year. And each time he asks me, with a twinkle in his eye, "Did I remove that gallbladder?" I nod. And he says, "Damn right. Skin to skin in less than two hours—without a brain. Not bad for a general surgeon."

Author's Note

There is no single entirely satisfactory review of transient global amnesia. The interested reader could start with the following:

Caplan, L. B. "Transient Global Amnesia." *Handbook of clinical neurology,* ed. P. J. Vinken, G. W. Bruyn, and H. L. Klawans, Vol. 45: 205–218. Amsterdam: Elsevier, 1985.

3
Wapniarka

His name was Mauritz Berg. Originally from Rumania, he'd come to Chicago in 1949, by way of Israel. He'd never legally changed his first name, but everyone now called him Morris or Mo.

I was not the physician who had diagnosed Morris's condition, and I never even bothered to confirm it. He told me his story and his diagnosis. Later he told me his other problems, and I tried to help him any way I could.

He was sixty-two when I first saw him as a patient in the early 1980s. I watched him struggle out of the chair in the waiting room when I called his name. He used two well-worn wooden canes similar to those my grandfather had used. I pointed the way to the examining room and stood there and observed him. He did not lift his legs at the hip the way a person with an intact nervous system does.

For most of us, walking is simple. We conceive of taking a step with our right foot and automatically, unconsciously, we shift our weight from our right to our left leg. We flex our right hip, lifting the right foot up off the floor. The right leg ad-

29

vances forward to hit the floor and once again begins to support some of the body's weight. And so it goes, step after step, unconsciously and effortlessly.

Not for Mr. Berg. He could shift his weight from one side to the other, but as he transferred weight to his left leg, it remained planted stiffly against the floor, and his left hip moved inward and downward in an exaggerated manner. At the same time his powerful arms and shoulders pushed down on those two wooden canes. His right hip did not bend at all. Instead his leg moved out in a semicircular pathway. His hip did not flex, his knees were locked in a partly bent position, and his foot did not actually lift up off the floor. His heel did lift perhaps an inch or two at the most, but his toes never did; they were just dragged along by the rotary motion of his hip and the strength of his upper body.

His next step, with his left leg, was identical. In that way he dragged and scraped himself into my examining room.

What I had just observed was a specific form of gait disorder that is due to disease or dysfunction in one specific subsystem of the nervous system. The dysfunction is called *circumduction*: to lead around in a circular or, more correctly, semicircular fashion. This disorder is due to an abnormality in the pathway that controls voluntary motor movements. This pathway begins in the brain itself in a strip of cerebral cortex that stretches along the back of the frontal lobe and is cleverly called the *motor* or *precentral cortex*. The latter term is derived from the anatomical fact that this cortex is immediately in front of the central sulcus or division. This area has a functional arrangement; the different parts of the body are represented in specific locations within this strip of the brain.

The large neurons of the precentral cortex are often called *Betz cells* after the anatomist who first described them. The axons of these large Betz cells come together deep inside each hemisphere to form a tract of nerve fibers called the *pyramidal tract*. When it reaches the lowest level of the brain stem, the pyramidal tract decussates, or crosses, to the opposite side of the nervous system in order to enter the spinal cord. This is the pathway along which one side of the brain controls the movement of the opposite side of the body.

As in normal people, Mr. Berg's attempt to move his right leg began with activity in the Betz cells of his left motor cortex. These cells, which control movement in the opposite leg and hip, should have sent a message that traveled deep inside his left brain, through his left brain stem and into the pyramidal tract, and then across into the right side of his spinal cord. In the spinal cord, the fibers of the pyramidal tract stimulate the motor cells of the spinal cord. These then generate impulses that act directly upon the appropriate muscles to cause the precise movement that the brain wanted to initiate. It goes like this:

1. The idea to move is generated in the brain or *frontal lobe*.
2. This idea then initiates activity in the *motor cortex*.
3. This activity then travels down the *pyramidal tract*.
4. The activity enters the opposite side of the spinal cord in order to stimulate the *spinal motor neurons*.
5. The impulses from these cells travel to the specific muscles to cause those movements that we call walking. They stimulate the muscles of the *hip* to result in *flexion*, the *knee* to result in *flexion*, and the *ankle* and *foot* to result in *elevation*.

In Mr. Berg this process had gone haywire. But where had it gone wrong? A neurological problem anywhere in this system could interrupt the process and prevent normal walking.

Could the problem have been inside his frontal lobe? No. Disease in the frontal lobe itself causes an inability to initiate the entire process. The patient cannot transmit to the motor cortex the unconscious concept of walking. But Mr. Berg could and did do that. He tried to walk and *did* walk. It was the characteristics of his walking that were abnormal. Therefore his frontal lobe generated the idea of walking and got that concept to the motor cortex.

Could the problem be with the motor cortex? No. The motor cortex generated a signal to walk. It was just that that signal did not get through normally.

That left two possible sites for his difficulty: the pyramidal tract and the spinal motor neurons. These two clinical situations are easy to tell apart. Injury to the pyramidal tract causes spasticity, a condition in which the muscles are stiff or spastic, having increased tone. In spasticity the weakness is not universal; all of the muscles of the affected arm or leg are not equally weak. Instead the weakness follows a peculiar pattern: The hip cannot flex (bend forward), but it can still circumduct (move laterally along a circular pathway). The knee does not flex, but it can lock and support weight. The foot drags. In contrast, abnormalities of the spinal cord neurons cause weakness and muscle wasting with no spasticity and no ability to lock the knee and support the body.

The signs of injury to the pyramidal tract describe Mr. Berg's gait perfectly. He manifested the classic signs of spastic circumduction, which occurs only in disease of the pyramidal tract. By watching him shuffle toward my examining room I therefore knew that Mr. Berg, at age sixty-two, had two lesions of the pyramidal tract. One led from his left motor cortex to the right side of his spinal cord. The lesion of the opposite pyramidal tract led from his right motor cortex to the left side of his spinal cord.

And where along the length of the pyramidal tract was the site of difficulty? That I also knew. His problem was located somewhere in the spinal cord itself.

Why? Because his arms were spared. They were strong—probably stronger than normal because he used them to pull his legs forward. Hence the disease struck his two pyramidal tracts only after they sent their appropriate messages to the spinal motor neurons, which innervated the muscles of his arms and then wended their way farther down the spinal cord to the cells that would move his leg muscles. Mr. Berg had something wrong with the two pyramidal tracts inside his spinal cord between his arms and his legs.

When had it started? What had caused it? Those were the questions I supposed he had come to ask me, but I was wrong. He already knew the answers.

He sat down rather heavily in one of the chairs in the examining room. It had been hard work for him, and he was breathing deeply. I waited for him to catch his breath before I started asking him the litany of questions that had already formed inside my brain. The list of possible causes—the differential diagnosis—of spastic paraparesis (that is what his problem is called) is a long one. So I had to ask many questions. The list includes everything from tumors of the spinal cord and multiple sclerosis to amyotrophic lateral sclerosis and pernicious anemia. The longer the list of possible diseases, the more facts I have to learn from the patient to arrive at the correct diagnosis, and therefore the more questions I have to ask.

He signaled that he was ready by asking me, "Can you help me?"

"That depends on what's wrong with you."

"You saw that already, I assume."

I nodded. "But I do not know the cause."

"Ah," he said. Then he added a single word. "Wapniarka."

"What?"

"Wapniarka," he said once again. It was as if that word should have explained everything.

It didn't—not to me at least.

He looked down at his hands. They were remarkably deformed. The knuckles were grossly enlarged at the joints, disfigured so that not a single finger was straight. Each segment of each finger seemed to have its own direction. It was if someone had intentionally displaced each joint, distorting nature's original plan. "Wapniarka," he said a third time.

"I don't understand."

"Understand! Who understands?" In his anger, I could detect an accent I recognized—a Yiddish accent. "I don't understand," he continued. "I never will. But you should know. You are a bright man, I'm told. A world expert. An important neurologist. You must know. It must be known." So he told me.

It had begun on September 16, 1942.

I had been five years old then, just entering kindergarten. But what he had entered was far from being a kindergarten.

He was nineteen years old and living in Bucharest when he became one of twelve hundred Rumanian Jews, all young, strong, healthy men who were rounded up and taken to Wapniarka, a small town in the Ukraine, and put into a forced labor camp run by the Ukrainians for the Nazis. Not a healthy place for Jews, that much I knew.

"Do you want details?" he asked.

I did. Neurologists are obsessed by details; we flourish on them. Mr. Berg considered the learning and transmission of these details a sacred obligation, and he knew them well. He had been in medical school when the Nazis invaded Rumania. He had wanted to be a surgeon. He looked at his hands again, as did I. He laughed a grotesque laugh. I didn't laugh at all.

He began again. Twelve hundred Jews, young, healthy, and capable of doing a full day's work: fourteen hours, sixteen hours, eighteen hours, rarely less. And they had been put on a diet of *Lathyrus sativus*.

"Lath . . . ," I started to repeat.

"Chickling peas," he said, cutting off my interruption. I did not interrupt him again.

The daily ration for each of them consisted of 400 grams of *Lathyrus sativus*, or chickling peas, cooked in salt water, plus 200 grams of bread made from barley and hay.

Mr. Berg no longer sounded like a patient telling his own story. He was a historian reciting facts, facts that any intelligent person should want to know—an important story, one that had to be told.

Beginning in December of 1942, less than three months after they had arrived in Wapniarka, the Jews began to have symptoms. Always the same, they began with spasms and weakness in the legs.

"How many had these symptoms?" I asked.

"Eight hundred." Two-thirds. "Mostly those who were most malnourished, but even some of us who were not yet half starved to death."

Some 150 Ukrainians and Russians were also in the camp. They had been there before the arrival of the Jews and had been fed a diet of 200 grams of chickling peas each day plus the barley-hay bread for six months or more. None of them had developed leg weakness. After the Jews arrived and the ration of chickling peas was increased, the Ukrainians and Russians also came down with the disease, some as early as November.

Mr. Berg remembered one of them well. He was a Russian Jew. The Ukrainian camp guards had not known that; they merely thought he was a communist. He and Mr. Berg talked together often in Yiddish. They had both been medical students. The Russian had a rapidly spreading paralysis. First his legs, then his arms, then he developed difficulty with his speech, and finally he had trouble swallowing.

I knew the outcome. Mr. Berg told me nonetheless, and I listened intently, for I wanted to learn all of the details: pneumonia, heart failure, death.

And so it went on, day after day, week after week. First one man became sick, then a few more. Then dozens. Then scores. Eventually, hundreds of Mr. Berg's fellow slave laborers became ill. For each of them, the illness was a little different—each had his own history of symptoms—yet they had the same overall clinical picture. All of them developed spasms and weakness, beginning in the legs and spreading up the body, becoming more and more severe. In some the process was fast, in others it was slow. Some went on to develop gangrene; others didn't. A few had seizures, convulsions, and many of them died. But not all.

The first cases of the paralysis were among the Rumanian Jews who ate their full daily rations and sometimes even more. They were expected to put in a hard day's work, so they had to eat, and there were plenty of chickling-peas to be eaten. The peas of *Lathyrus sativus* yielded enough calories and proteins to sustain humans in a reasonably well-nourished state to keep them working at hard labor fourteen or more hours a day. The Ukrainians of Wapniarka were malicious bastards (*Mumzers*, the Yiddish word for bastards, was the word Mr. Berg used), and they had work that had to get done and Jews to do it.

Mr. Berg helped one of the doctors—yes, there were doctors among the twelve hundred Rumanian Jews—document and study what was happening to them. That was before the doctor himself got the disease and before Mr. Berg also came down with it. But they survived, and after the Holocaust, he and the doctor continued their documentation.

In the camp, Mr. Berg and the doctor meticulously recorded the manifestations of the disease. It was this physician, Dr. Kessler, who first recognized that the disease causing paralysis in the prisoners was a specific disease called *lathyrism*. It almost always began in the same way, with painful muscle spasms in the extremities that lasted for seconds or minutes and were especially bothersome at night. After one month of continuous consumption of the diet of chickling peas, as early as October 1942, some of the victims were unable to maintain bladder function and urinated thirty to forty times during the night. The victims next began to have difficulty walking. Their walking became unstable, and by the end of December spastic paraparesis appeared in the lower extremities, and severely affected individuals rapidly became bedridden. The men could no longer do hard labor.

Once Dr. Kessler recognized the cause, he told the powers that be. They changed the diet, stopping the consumption of *L. sativus* on January 22, 1943. No more cases of the paralysis appeared. By February, bladder problems in some of the men changed from an inability to control spontaneous emptying to some degree of retention with dribbling. In most of them the muscle cramps abated to some degree, but the lower extremities remained weak and spastic.

Mr. Berg, just another one of these victims, relayed his own detailed clinical history to me. More than the unique story of one man's suffering, it mirrored the story of every inmate of Wapniarka—and many others who suffered in the Holocaust as well.

On September 16, 1942, Mauritz Berg began consuming the usual inmate diet of 400 grams of chickling peas and 200 grams of bread made from barley and hay. In December 1942, while the Russians were turning the tide of the war at Stalingrad, he began having spasms in his leg muscles, first in the calf muscles, then in the thighs. The spasms were especially prominent at night. Next he became aware of a burning sensation beginning in his feet and quickly spreading up his legs. Other symptoms followed in rapid succession: trouble holding his urine, progressive difficulty walking. This was mild at first but inexorably became more and more severe. By the end of January, it was all he could do to walk. That was when one of the guards called him a loafer and crushed his hands, one finger at a time, as an example to the other Jewish loafers who refused to work for their food.

When the diet was changed—they were fed fewer chickling peas and more hay, even a bit more barley—Mr. Berg's walking and control of his urine got somewhat better. The burning sensation and the spasms disappeared. He was left as he still was when he came to see me—with weak and spastic legs.

Could I help him?, he wanted to know. Were there any medicines that might loosen up his legs and make walking less of a burden? He was no longer young. He had some angina. Pulling his legs behind him was harder than it had once been.

Perhaps, I said. There was nothing to do about what had happened to him in 1942. He had eaten too many chickling peas, and doing that had damaged his nervous system. How or why no one knew, and I couldn't help. But he did have a particular type of neurological damage—spasticity—and there are some medications that sometimes help to decrease spasticity no matter what its cause. Those medications might help him a bit. As far as I knew, these medications had never been used in patients with spasticity due to lathyrism, but that should make no difference. Spasticity results from any disease that interrupts the normal transmission of impulses down the pyramidal tracts to the spinal motor neurons, so the spasticity is the same no matter what causes the interruption. It is almost as if the state of spasticity is the "normal" state of the spinal motor neurons if they are deprived of control of the brain. This loss of cortical or pyramidal tract control or inhibition is associated with increased spinal neuron activity, which we call spasticity. Some drugs seem to lessen this increased activity by inhibiting the neurons directed. Baclofen is one such agent, so I started Morris Berg on baclofen.

When I saw him two weeks later, he was better. He still circumducted his legs, but they moved more freely. He was less out of breath when he got to my examining room, and he did not fall into the chair. He was better, and he thanked me.

Morris Berg was the only patient with lathyrism I had ever personally seen and examined, but it was a classic disease I had known about since I'd been a first-year resident. I had known about it for years before I'd ever seen such a case. Had the Ukrainians? Had the Nazis? Between Mr. Berg's two visits to my office I went back to the books.

Lathyrism is not a new disease. It was known to the ancient Hindus. It was also known to Hippocrates (460–377 B.C.), who described it in his book *On Epidemic*: "At Ainos . . . all men and women, who ate continuously chickling peas became impotent in the legs and that state persisted." Lathyrism was also known to Pliny the Elder (A.D. 23–79), Galen (A.D. 130–210), and the Greek pharmacologist and physician Pedanius Dioskurides (b. A.D. 50).

But ancient history was not the question; European understanding and knowledge were. In 1671 Duke George of Württemberg banned consumption of lathyrus flour in his principality because of its "paralyzing effects on the legs." During the eighteenth, nineteenth, and twentieth centuries, outbreaks of lathyrism occurred throughout Europe, northern Africa, the Middle East, Afghanistan, Russia, and India. Its occurrence is so well known that no one—not Rumanians, not Germans, not Ukrainians—uses chickling peas as their major source of calories today.

The occurrence of major epidemics has been documented in regions of France (1700–1701 and the 1820s), Algiers (1883), Russia (1892), India (1829 and 1856), and Spain (the 1940s). Today, lathyrism is largely restricted to north-central India, Bangladesh, and Ethiopia, but the disease could return to other countries in conditions of war, famine, or imprisonment if humans or even other animals are forced to eat *Lathyrus* peas in order to survive.

The first detailed account of an outbreak of lathyrism is found in Sir William Henry Sleeman's *Rambles and Recollections of an Indian Official*:

In 1829, the wheat and other spring crops . . . were destroyed by severe hailstorms and rains; in 1830 they were deficient from the want of seasonable rains, and in 1831 they were destroyed by blight. During these three years the 'teori' or what in other parts of India is called 'kesari' (*L. sativus*), a kind of wild vetch which, though not sown itself, is left carelessly to grow among the wheat and other grains and given in the green and dry state to cattle, remained uninjured and thrived with great luxuriance. In 1831, they reaped a rich crop of it from the blighted wheat fields and subsisted upon its grain during that and the following years, giving the stalks and leaves only to their cattle. In 1833, the sad effects of this food began to manifest themselves. The younger part of the population of this and the surrounding villages, from the age of thirty downwards, began to be deprived of the use of their limbs below the waist by paralytic strokes, in all cases sudden, but in some cases more severe than others. About half the youth of this village of both sexes became affected during the year 1833–1834 and many of them have lost the use of their lower limbs entirely and are unable to move.

The term *lathyrism* was first used to describe this disorder in 1873 by the Italian physician Cantani. The disease had changed very little over the years. In 1929 Stockman published this description:

Sometimes there are prodromal sensory symptoms of pain, prickling, numbness and cramps, but most commonly the victim quite suddenly feels the legs and loins weak and heavy, the muscles are tremulous when weight is put on them, there is dragging of the legs, increased reflexes and more or less inability to walk. This may go on to a further stage of extreme spasticity and rigidity of the leg muscle; the gait becomes jerky with short steps taken on the balls of the feet and with the knees slightly flexed; . . . spasms of the thigh muscles are easily excited. . . . In a few cases the arms have been affected like the legs. It is said to be sometimes ushered in by convulsive movements of the upper and lower limbs and painful contraction of the muscles. . . . Early cases sometimes recover, others never.

The people in charge of Wapniarka definitely knew that eating chickling peas would cause something that wasn't good. It was part of the general knowledge in that part of Europe. The peasants all knew it so well that chickling peas were never used as a staple of the diet. Not for people, horses, cows, or even pigs. Just for Jews.

Once Dr. Kessler put the pieces together and made the correct diagnosis, the commandant of Wapniarka did not argue with him. He merely changed the diet for all of the slave laborers. The experiment was over.

In 1976 when I first saw Morris Berg, medical science knew that the use of chickling peas as the major source of nutrition caused spastic weakness of the legs, but *how* it did that was unclear. At first it was thought to be due to some peculiar deficiency, some necessary nutrient present in all foods but chickling peas. This theory seemed untenable, and long before the 1970s it was believed that lathyrism was due to some poison found within the chickling peas. But what poison? When Mr. Berg first became my patient, I had no idea.

I continued to see Mr. Berg about once every six months. Over the years, his neurological disease changed very little. Every once in a while, I adjusted his medicine. His mangled hands never changed either. But his heart disease got worse— more angina, more chest pain on less and less effort.

The last time I saw him, he told me a new story. He had just been examined by a physician, an American who was under contract to the West German government. That government has granted disability pensions to some of the survivors of the Holocaust. The job of this physician was to examine such individuals periodically in order to determine whether those who were receiving such disability payments because of injuries that occurred during World War II still deserved their disability allowances. The physician had been careful to say "World War II" and not "the Holocaust."

Mr. Berg told the doctor about all of his symptoms. He told him about his hands—after all, he had traumatic arthritis of both hands that had been initiated when his hands had been crushed by the guard. He also told the doctor about his lathyrism, his spastic paraparesis, and his angina.

The doctor examined Mr. Berg carefully and told him his findings. Mr. Berg's major problem was his angina. Not his hands, not his spinal cord. His angina. The doctor would report that, and his monthly check would be reduced.

"I have these nightmares," Mr. Berg told the physician. And he did—horrid, grotesque, frightening nightmares. He'd had them ever since his hands had been crushed. Other victims had had such dreams from the lathyrism itself.

"We don't pay for dreams," the doctor said.

We don't pay for dreams.

Mr. Berg died about six months later of a heart attack.

Today we finally understand the cause of the spastic paraparesis of lathyrism. That understanding never helped Mr. Berg, or any of his fellow prisoners, dead or alive.

Under any condition, when the chickling pea makes up as much as two-thirds of the diet, humans develop lathyrism. Domestic animals given L. sativus as fodder also develop limb paralysis. Epidemics of this have occurred in many countries, including the United States and Britain. Lathyrism has been reported in ducks, geese, hens, peacocks, pigs, oxen, sheep, and elephants, but the horse has most commonly been poisoned and appears most susceptible to Lathyrus intoxication. In horses, a diet consisting exclusively of L. sativus reportedly precipitates signs after approximately ten days, whereas animals fed only one or two quarts a day develop the disease after two to three months, and neurological manifestations may appear a month or more after the peas have been withdrawn from the diet. The signs consist of paralysis of the hind legs as well as difficulty breathing.

If that is the scenario needed to cause lathyrism, the disease should be quite simple to study. All that should be necessary is to feed chickling-peas to laboratory animals. However, attempts to induce spastic paraparesis in laboratory animals fed L. sativus have rarely succeeded. Early reports of success using various animal species were poorly documented and not reproduced by subsequent investigators.

This contrast is perplexing. Lathyrism occurred in nature but not in the laboratory. In part this may have reflected the species' differences in response to eating *Lathyrus* peas. Whatever was causing the problem affected certain species more than others, humans and horses more than rats and guinea pigs. As a result, spastic paraparesis had been induced in only a few experiments.

Even the successful production of paralysis in experimental animals did not prove precisely what caused the paralysis. Over the years, several compounds found in *Lathyrus* plants have been proposed to be the cause of human lathyrism only to be disproved later. In recent years interest has focused on beta-(N)-oxalyl-L-alanine (BOAA), a so-called neurotoxic amino acid present in *L. sativus* species in concentrations of 0.2 to 2.5 percent. It was a far better candidate than the other chemicals already studied and discarded, for it has acute neurotoxic properties, is present in those species of *Lathyrus* known to induce the disease, and is absent in those not causally associated with lathyrism.

It was Peter Spencer, a pathologist at Albert Einstein Medical School in New York, and his associates who finally solved the riddle. They produced a model of lathyrism in male macaques by first feeding them *Lathyrus sativus* and later feeding other monkeys BOAA itself. A consistent pattern of abnormal neurological signs appeared in all animals. Affected animals showed a fine tremor, periodic myoclonic-like jerks, mild-to-moderate increased muscle tone of the leg, and a striking hind-limb posturing characteristic of macaques with surgically induced pyramidal tract lesions in the spinal cord.

By feeding these animals excessive amounts of BOAA the researchers had produced the symptoms of lathyrism. Furthermore, the changes they saw in the animals were comparable to those seen in human lathyrism. The changes in the Betz cells and spinal cords of Spencer's monkeys were much like the changes seen in one of Mr. Berg's fellow prisoners who had died in 1977. This meant that we now knew the precise cause of lathyrism: poisoning by a specific chemical, BOAA.

Had we known that before he died, the knowledge wouldn't have helped Morris Berg. The damage had been done long ago. Besides, lathyrism is an obscure disease caused by peculiar dietary problems and prevented by not eating chickling peas. Why should we care if we know which precise poison it is, or even that it is a particular toxin at all?

Because finally understanding what killed the cells in Spencer's macaques as well as the Jews of Wapniarka has opened up a new way of thinking about diseases of the brain and spinal cord, diseases we used to classify as either degenerative or without known cause or treatment. That was how we used to classify lathyrism: a disease of unknown cause. Today we know the cause. There are many other neurologic diseases now classified as diseases of unknown cause. In many of these, the changes we see in the brain or spinal cord resemble the changes symptomatic of lathyrism. Perhaps some of these diseases may also be due to a toxin, and if so we may be able someday to devise ways to prevent the toxicity and the disease it causes.

This is not just an idle wish. It has already proved to be true. The first disease is one that is rarer than lathyrism and even more obscure. It is a disease that includes the features of Parkinson's disease, Alzheimer's disease, and amytrophic lateral sclerosis (ALS, better known as Lou Gehrig's disease) in varying proportions. It has been best documented among the indigenous people of Guam, the Chamorros. It is sometimes called ALS if that is the predominant feature, or parkinson-dementia if parkinsonism and dementia are the major features.

Surveys conducted in the early 1950s demonstrated that about 10 percent of deaths among adult Chamorros living in Guam resulted from this form of ALS combined with parkinsonism. This is a rate about a hundred times greater than in the population of the United States. However, during the past thirty years, the prevalence of the Guam disease has dropped steadily. The progressive decline of ALS-parkinsonism in Guam has coincided with the westernization of Guam. This observation has suggested that some vanishing environmental factor causes this disease. Two hypotheses have stimulated major interest. The first suggested that some peculiar mineral deficiency resulted in metal intoxication; the second hypothesis was that Parkinson-dementia and ALS were both due to poisoning by a dietary toxin.

The latter hypothesis centers on the consumption of the toxic seed of *Cycas circinalis* (the falso sago palm). This species of cycad is distributed throughout western Pacific regions where there is a high prevalence of ALS–Parkinson-dementia, and it represented a major source of carbohydrates for the Guamanian people before their post–World War II westernization. The role of cycad in Guam ALS–Parkinson-dementia excited much research interest between 1963 and 1973 because of reports that cattle grazing on Australian cycads frequently developed gait disturbances, motor weakness, and paralysis, a condition similar to what happens when horses are fed chickling peas. Most laboratory efforts focused on cycasin, a cycad component that proved to be a potent liver toxin and carcinogen. However, cycasin was not shown to induce experimental motor neuron disease, and the cycad hypothesis fell into disrepute. Since we did not yet know that lathyrism was caused by BOAA, there was absolutely no scientific interest in a related chemical long known to exist in cycad, beta-N-methylamino-L-alanine (BMAA).

BMAA chemically resembles BOAA. The analogy was obvious, and once again it was Peter Spencer and his associates who supplied the needed evidence. They proved that BMAA could and did cause chronic motor system toxin in primates. Repeated oral administration of synthetic BMAA (125–315 mg/kg daily) to male macaques over weeks or months induced signs of pyramidal dysfunction in the extremities, limb weakness, wrist drop and tremor, parkinsonism, a masklike face, and behavioral changes.

So what? What difference does it make if we know what causes two obscure diseases rather than just one? Perhaps none, perhaps a great deal.

A Chamorro eats cycads in 1940. He gets his disease in 1960. His disease can be similar to ALS or Parkinson's disease. Very similar. Could some form of ALS be due to a toxin? Could Parkinson's disease? We don't know.

For generations we have called these diseases "degenerative." But we've never known why the nerve cells degenerated. Perhaps they were poisoned. We do not know.

As Peter Spencer himself said in discussing the possible roles of different poisons in various neurological diseases, "We have to be prepared to look under some very unlikely stones." After all, the gateway to understanding the Guam disease was via Wapniarka and Mauritz Berg and his fellow victims of what seemed at the time to be just another twentieth-century atrocity.

AUTHOR'S NOTE

The story of the labor camp at Wapniarka and the lathyrism that developed there was first told by the physician-victim who made the correct diagnosis:

Kessler, A. "Lathyrismus." *Mschr. Psychiat. Neurol.* 113: 348 (1947).

Two follow-up studies of many of these patients have been published:

Cohn, D. F., and M. Streifler. "Human neurolathyrism, a follow-up study of 200 patients, Part 1." *Arch. Suisses Neurol., Neuroch. Psychiat.* 128: 141 (1981).

Cohn, D. F., and M. Streifler. "Human lathyrism, a follow-up study, Part 2." *Arch. Suisses Neurol. Neuroch. Psychiat.* 128: 157 (1981).

There also have been two studies of the pathology of one of the victims:

Streifler, M., D. F. Cohn, A. Hirano and E. Schujman. "The central nervous system in neurolathyrism." *Neurology* 27: 1,176 (1977).

Hirano, A., J. F. Llena, M. Streifler, and D. F. Cohn. "Anterior horn cell changes in a case of neurolathyrism." *Acta Neuropathol.* 35: 277 (1976).

Summaries of the work of Peter Spencer and his colleagues, as well as all the others who contributed to this story, can also be found in two places:

Spencer, P., J. Hugen, A. Ludolph, P. B. Nunn, S. M. Ross, D. N. Roy, and H. H. Schaumburg. "Discovery and partial characterization of primate motor system toxins." *Selective Neuronal Death. Ciba Foundation Symposium 126*, 221–238. New York: John Wiley & Sons, 1987.

Spencer, P. S., H. H. Schaumburg, D. F. Cohn, and P. K. Seth. "Lathyrism: a useful model of primary lateral sclerosis." *Research Progress in Motor Neuron Disease*, ed. F. Rose, 312–327. London: Pitman Medical Publishers, 1984.

I thank Peter Spencer for taking the time to review this chapter.

Perhaps the most interesting sidelight to this story has to do not with lathyrism or ALS or even the ALS–Parkinson-dementia of Guam, but with Parkinson's disease itself. In 1982 a group of young heroin addicts near Santa Cruz, California, encountered yet another poison, in this case under the guise of a new "synthetic heroin." Instead of the expected high, these users found themselves developing all the signs and symptoms of classic Parkinson's disease. The identity of the toxin was quickly discovered. It's known as MPTP, and it can cause Parkinson's disease in humans and a variety of other animals.

Does that mean that Parkinson's disease, which was always thought of as a degenerative disease, is really a toxic disease due to MPTP or some related chemical? And if it is, are there drugs that can prevent the toxicity? After all, there are drugs that can prevent MPTP from causing parkinsonism in monkeys. Will the same medicine that prevents MPTP from causing parkinsonism in monkeys prevent Parkinson's disease in humans from progressing? It's unknown. But now, for the first time, we can at least study whether or not we can prevent the progression of a so-called degenerative disease.

It is not a simple question to answer. A five-year research project funded by the National Institutes of Health began in April 1987. Leading it are Ira Shoulson of the University of Rochester and Stanley Fahn of the New York Neurologic Institute.

In October 1986 Elie Wiesel received the Nobel Peace Prize. He is the first recipient of that prize whose major role has been to be a public witness to what others had experienced during the Holocaust and recalled only privately. It is unfortunately true that no one pays for dreams. Or nightmares. But those who suffer them have an obligation to humanity not to hide them. And those of us who learn their stories have the same obligation. I hope I have begun to live up to that obligation.

4

The Man Who Would Save the World

John Lipon was a pediatrician. More accurately, he had been a pediatrician. When he first came to see me he was fifty-eight years old and had been unable to practice medicine for two years. He had had Parkinson's disease for five or six. Neither the medicines he'd been given nor the surgery he had undergone had helped him. The year was 1969, and he needed a miracle to save him. He was convinced that L-dopa would be that miracle and that I would be the one who would preside over its occurrence.

Why me? That was one of the first questions I asked Dr. Lipon when I saw him for the first time in my office. He lived in Tacoma, Washington, and I practiced medicine in Chicago. Why had he traveled well over two thousand miles to see me? I was not the only physician in the country using L-dopa to treat Parkinson's disease, and I was certainly not the best known. I was barely out of my residency. There had to be someone who was closer to his home who had governmental clearance to administer L-dopa—someone in Seattle or Portland, Oregon, or even Vancouver. Dr. Lipon's answer seemed reasonable enough: He had gone to medical school in Chicago, taken his residency at the hospital where I worked, and still had many friends in Chicago. Since no one in Tacoma was authorized to administer L-dopa, he had to travel somewhere to be treated, so he chose Chicago.

His line of reasoning made perfect sense to me. In 1969 L-dopa was still an experimental medication. Only twenty or thirty physicians had obtained the right to study it in the treatment of Parkinson's disease. I was one of them, and Dr. Lipon had friends in Chicago.

I went on to ask him all the other questions that physicians ordinarily ask patients and all those added questions that were necessitated by the nature of his specific needs and the experimental status of L-dopa. The experimental use of any drug must follow a specific protocol. Each protocol has rigid inclusion criteria that must be met in order to include the patient in the study. In addition, a set of specific exclusion criteria, if present, excludes a patient who otherwise fulfills the inclusion criteria.

John Lipon had Parkinson's disease. That, of course, was the primary inclusion criterion. I was studying L-dopa in Parkinson's disease per se, not in any other disease, no matter how closely related.

None of the reasons for excluding a patient from the study applied to Dr. Lipon. He was significantly disabled but not so devastated that the medication was unlikely to do him much good. And he had no past history of any other significant disease that might interfere with my treatment of him. There was no past history of heart or liver disease. And, more specifically, there was no history of any major psychiatric disease. Thus, his answers to my many questions made him an appropriate candidate for L-dopa.

His demeanor struck me as a bit strange. Many patients came in expecting a miracle; very few, however, personalized that miracle the way he did or make it seem quite so miraculous.

I paid no attention; I was performing miracles every day. I was not raising people from the grave, but people who had not gotten out of wheelchairs by themselves in months or years were walking again. Perhaps it was not as miraculous as Elijah breathing life back into the body of the son of the Shulamite woman, but it wasn't bad for someone who had finished his residency only months earlier.

Don't get me wrong. I knew that these miraculous events were not due to *me*. They were due to a small, rather ordinary chemical called L-dopa. L-dopa had first been tried in parkinsonism in the early 1960s. Its use was not the result of serendipity or a lucky guess, as had been the case in the development of many other agents used in neurology. On the contrary, it was a logical extension of our scientific knowledge.

And it was far more than that. It was the beginning of a revolution. Neurology has long been the domain of anatomists and physiologists. The anatomists had named the parts of the brain and followed the various pathways. The physiologists had tried to define precisely what each of these parts did or, more correctly, what the brain could not do when each part was injured in some way. Chemists had measured this substance or that, but no one paid very much attention to either the neurochemists or the substances they measured. Then along came Parkinson's disease and brain dopamine and L-dopa.

L-dopa is a naturally occurring substance—an amino acid, one of the building blocks of the body's proteins. It also plays a role in the formation of a number of chemicals in the brain and elsewhere in the body. Two of these, dopamine and norepinephrine (adrenalin), are neurotransmitters, the simple chemicals that nerves use to transmit their messages to other nerves.

The process works this way: L-dopa is a precursor of dopamine. Certain specific cells within the brain, called dopaminergic (or dopamine-containing) neurons, manufacture dopamine from L-dopa. The process follows this pathway:

Tyrosine ⟶ L-Dopa ⟶ Dopamine

Normally the process starts with tyrosine, not L-dopa. Tyrosine is another amino acid, and it is much more prevalent in our diets than L-dopa. The key is dopamine, one of the "new" substances that neurochemists began to measure in the late 1950s.

The cells that manufacture and use about 80 to 90 percent of all the dopamine of the brain are the cells of the substantia nigra—a small collection of nerve cells deep in the brain stem. As I've mentioned before, it is the death of these cells that causes Parkinson's disease. This fact has been known since the early part of this century. But in the early 1960s Oleh Hornekiewicz, a pharmacologist working in Vienna, discovered that patients who died with Parkinson's disease had lost most of the dopamine from the areas of the brain that were thought to play a role in the control of movement.

This discovery was as startling as it was simple. One specific chemical was lost in the brains of patients who had Parkinson's disease. No other chemical then known was missing from these brains, and dopamine didn't seem to be lost in patients dying of other diseases. The revolution had started. Not with a bang, but with more than a whimper.

Since dopamine acts as a neurotransmitter, a chemical that carries messages from one set of cells to another, it was possible that the disruption of these messages is what causes the symptoms of Parkinson's disease. And, more significantly, restoration of dopamine activity within the brain might improve the clinical manifestations of Parkinson's disease.

The scientific reasoning was really no more complicated than that. Dopamine, which carried the messages from the cells of the substantia nigra to certain important structures (especially one called the striatum), was lost. It was lost because these cells were diseased and had died. There was nothing we could do about that. But perhaps we could overcome the problems caused by the death of these cells by somehow pumping dopamine into the brain.

How could we do it? Not by giving the patients dopamine itself, because dopamine cannot cross into the brain. The next logical candidate was L-dopa.

So in 1961 André Barbeau, a neurologist from Montreal, gave L-dopa to some patients with Parkinson's disease and reported improvement. The same year Birkmayer, a Viennese neurologist working with Hornekiewicz, made the same discovery. Research really got moving about five years later when the American George Cotzias was able to give larger doses of L-dopa to Parkinson's patients continuously over a period of months and demonstrated a marked, sustained benefit in a small group of patients.

That was where we stood, more or less, in 1969. I told all of that to Dr. Lipon. I also told him that I would be willing to try L-dopa on him but that I could make no promises. One could not promise to perform a miracle; promises and miracles resided in separate planes of existence.

But he did not require any promises. He agreed to enter the hospital so that we could initiate the attempt at a miracle. I gave him an informed-consent form to read and sign. He signed it without reading it. After all, one could not define the limitations of any miraculous event on a simple photocopied form.

"How long will I be in the hospital?" he asked.

"The average is about four weeks."

He seemed disappointed by my answer.

"Too short?" I asked rather jokingly. No one liked being in a hospital for a month.

"Too long," he replied.

"Well, you can't expect a miracle overnight."

He looked at me strangely as if he were gauging my understanding of what was about to transpire. After sizing me up, he concluded that I had come up short. "One cannot predict how long a miracle will take."

"With most miracles, you're undoubtedly right. But I've used L-dopa many times. . . ."

"How old are you?" he interrupted.

"Thirty-one."

He nodded condescendingly. Obviously, I had a great deal to learn.

He entered the hospital the next Sunday night, and I saw him on my regular hospital rounds on Monday morning. His tremor was more prominent than it had been four days before in my office. I had expected that. When he entered the hospital, we had stopped giving him the medications he was on in order to start the L-dopa. Those medications had probably been doing him some good, so stopping them should have made his parkinsonism worse. But the effects of stopping usually took a few days to manifest themselves.

"Your tremor is worse," I observed.

His words came out softly and hesitantly. "I . . . stopped my medicine. . . ."

"When?"

"I . . . threw them out . . . when . . . I . . . left your . . . office."

That explained his deterioration. It had not taken place overnight; he had been off his medication for four days. "Your voice is also worse," I added.

"No . . . matter . . . I will be better soon." He was probably right. He would be somewhat more uncomfortable for a few days, but in the long run this increase in his symptoms would make no difference.

It was not just his voice and tremor that were worse. All of his Parkinsonian symptoms were more marked. That made his disease more dramatic to the residents and students who were making rounds with me. Once I had shown him off to them, I told Dr. Lipon that his blood tests were all normal. "We'll start the L-dopa right after lunch."

"Boys," he said in a strong, confident voice, ignoring or excluding the one female medical student, "We are going to make medical history, Dr. K and I. Medical history."

When rounds were over, one of the medical students, the young woman, asked me if that was true. She wanted to know if Dr. Lipon and I were going to make medical history.

"Not really," I said. "The history has already been made. By Barbeau, and Birkmayer, and Cotzias."

"Isn't he . . . kind of . . . crazy?"

"No," I laughed. "In a way he's right. He will be part of history. What happens to him on L-dopa will be part of the data that will be supplied to the FDA in order to obtain approval for the general use of L-dopa in Parkinson's disease."

She nodded.

"So he is making history. Not like Ike or Omar Bradley, but like one of the GIs who landed on the beaches at Normandy. It's part of history but the only part that most people ever play. And no one remembers those people except their families and friends."

Dr. Lipon got his first dose of L-dopa that Monday at 12:30, immediately after lunch. I started him on 250 mg three times a day after meals. Most patients required three or four times that much or even more in order to obtain maximum benefit from the drug. And most patients did not even begin to improve until they were on L-dopa for a week or so.

The next day, Dr. Lipon's tremor was no better, nor was his walking. I had not expected him to show any response. But he had; his face was more animated, his eyes brighter, his voice stronger.

"How are you?" I asked.

"Waiting," he said.

"You must be patient. I told you it wouldn't happen overnight."

"But I have things I must do."

"And you will do them, but not today." I had no idea what he had to do, and I didn't particularly care. We all have things to do, things we think are very important. When he improved, he could do them.

On Friday we increased his dose to 500 mg after each meal, a total of 1,500 mg each day. On the next Monday when we made rounds, Dr. Lipon was no longer sitting in a chair, relatively immobile. He was walking around his room. He was not pacing and did not seem to be abnormally restless. He was just walking as if he were strolling and contemplating some major philosophical issue—not Sherlock Holmes stalking Moriarty, but Socrates in a garden.

"You're better," I said giving neither him nor the residents and students any information that they had not already grasped on their own.

He did not respond.

"John," I said, "you're better."

"Yes, yes. We knew that would happen."

We didn't. Not really, although the odds were with him. Not every patient with Parkinson's disease responded to L-dopa—and certainly not to so small a dose, or so quickly, or so dramatically.

"There are more important things on my mind."

I was sure there were. I would let him wrestle with them first. The issues were obvious. How much of a miracle would occur? One hundred percent improvement? Or fifty? Or in between. How long would it last? Could he go back to practice? Could he once again be an active physician? If so, how soon?

Before I could answer his questions, he would need time to formulate them, and I would need more time to observe him and his responses. I was in no hurry to have to answer his questions, so I said nothing.

The next day he no longer resembled Socrates in a garden. Perhaps he reminded me most of Maigret—not the calm Maigret at the outset of an investigation, but the agitated Maigret knowing he had learned the secret but unsure of what it meant, how to piece it all together, where to go next, what to do next, who to pursue, who to question, what bistro to visit. Once more Dr. Lipon was in no mood to talk. He paced the room continuously while I asked him my routine questions. His answers were all brief, abrupt, telegraphic.

How was he?

Better.

What was better?

Everything.

Did the medicine bother him?

No.

Was he bothered by anything at all?

No. No.

Why was he pacing?

He was thinking about the future.

I would, I decided, give him a few more days to think about it, and then we would sit down together and have a discussion.

On Wednesday he was not in his room. He was in the hallway, walking up and down. His gait was rapid with long strides and his arms swung freely at his sides in a normal fashion. He turned rapidly, pivoting as if he had no disease at all. His improvement was far closer to 100 percent than to 50 percent.

I called to him. He continued walking. I fell into pace beside him, and we went through the usual questions. His answers were unchanged from the day before, yet his demeanor was different. He was even more preoccupied—not agitated or anxious but detached from the mundane issues of medications, side effects, hospital routine, and even therapeutic benefits. I got the sense that he wanted to talk to me.

"Do you have any questions?" I asked.

"No."

"Do you want to talk to me?"

"Yes."

I waited. We walked up the hall and back, up and back. I asked him what was on his mind.

"The future," he said.

"I'm here to talk to you," I reminded him.

"So are they."

They? I understood. The students and resident with whom I made rounds had all fallen into step right behind us.

"Should I come back later?"

"Yes."

"Alone?"

"Alone."

By the time I finished rounds and returned to talk to him, it was after lunch. He was still pacing in the hallway. Once again I caught up with him. He looked around, making sure that none of the students or residents were with me. None were.

"You wanted to talk to me," I said.

"Not here."

"Where?"

"In my room."

A good choice. I had been making rounds for four hours. I felt like sitting down. We walked back to his room. His uneaten lunch was still there. I sat on the chair, but he continued to walk back and forth.

"Your lunch," I said.

"I'm not hungry."

I understood. L-dopa often caused some degree of nausea and loss of appetite, especially during the first few weeks of treatment. "Are you sure?" I persisted.

"I can't be bothered with food at a time like this."

I could. I uncovered the tray. He'd ordered macaroni and it was cold. I too felt a bit nauseated. "Tell me about your future."

"We can do great things," he began.

"We?"

"You and I," he explained.

"Great things?"

"Wondrous things. You will win a Nobel Prize."

"No. Not me. I don't do the kind of research that wins Nobel Prizes."

"Not in medicine. The real prize, the Nobel Peace Prize."

I was lost.

"We can do it. We will do it. It's our destiny, our role in history."

Our role in history? His and mine. What role was that? My fantasies had at times taken on grandiose aspects but never quite that grandiose. "How?" I asked.

"You still don't know. You still don't understand. You've had the power to perform this miracle for so long, this wondrous power, and you had no idea."

I still had no idea.

"You and I are going to save the world."

"How?" I repeated.

He stopped pacing and told me. The biggest threat to the world was the Chinese, he said—not the Russians but the Chinese, the Yellow Hordes led by Mao Tse-tung, the reincarnation of Fu Man Chu. And Chairman Mao was irascible and therefore unpredictable. And John Lipon knew why Mao was so irascible. The State Department didn't, Nixon certainly didn't, the Russians didn't. But John Lipon, retired pediatrician from Tacoma, Washington, knew precisely what made Mao Tse-tung tick.

Mao had Parkinson's disease, and if there was anything John Lipon knew and understood, it was Parkinson's disease. Not Parkinson's disease as a deficiency of dopamine in the striatum, not Parkinson's disease as an imbalance of neurotransmitters in the brain, but Parkinson's disease as a disease that gnawed away at a person's heart and soul. A disease that began as an irritation, a mild aggravation, a bother, an incumbrance, but that ultimately affected your way of life and became your way of life. Parkinson's disease that began by slowing your gait and then transformed you into a slow-motion caricature of your former self.

That was what Dr. Lipon knew that no one else did. Neither the United Nations, nor the State Department, nor the president knew, because they couldn't. They didn't have Parkinson's disease and he did, so he knew.

Parkinson's disease does not just make you slow; it does not just make you shake. It eats away at you. And, no matter what you were, you change. You can no longer laugh, play, or even smile. You can no longer overlook the slights of others, the insults, the plots, the maneuverings. You must protect yourself from them, for no one else will protect you.

The world sees you as irascible, recalcitrant, and rigid, but you have to be. What other choice is there? "Parkinson's disease," he said, "makes you that way. It's like having a constant itch in a place you can't reach, a scratch that gets worse and worse and will never go away. There is no relief, no respite. That is Mao. That was me."

"Was?" I asked.

"I no longer itch," he said. "I'm cured."

"Not cured. You are responding to treatment, but that treatment must be continued. If we stop it . . ."

"The itch will come back," he interrupted.

"Yes," I nodded.

He said nothing. He seemed to have exhausted himself. It was as if his brain had run out of energy.

I too had had itches I couldn't scratch. I could imagine how he must be feeling. It was an elation caused by a new feeling of normality that was preoccupying him, a sense of well-being. Or perhaps it was more an absence of ill-being. People who are healthy are unaware of their bodies; our bodies are but noiseless backdrops to our lives. Far from silent, his body had become a constant high-pitched interference pattern—a pattern that was now gone. He could once again play out his life in front of a backdrop. No wonder he walked ceaselessly, experiencing the joy of walking without having to battle his disease. And no wonder he wanted to share this miracle with others, even with Fu Man Chu in the guise of Mao Tse-tung.

"We can't go to China," I said.

"We must. We have to. We must save the world."

"Don't worry," I reassured him. "Someone will do it. Someone has, in all probability. The rumor in neurological circles is that both Barbeau and Birkmayer have been to China to see Mao."

John looked at me suspiciously as if to ask whether I was telling him the truth. I was. I repeated my reassurance, but John was not reassured.

"But my plan . . . what will I do? You . . . I. . . ." His voice got softer, more hesitant, interrupted—the speech of a patient with Parkinson's disease. "We . . . must save the world."

"Another day," I said. "Perhaps we'll go to Spain and treat Franco."

"Ah . . . Franco."

I went out of town and didn't get a chance to see Dr. Lipon again for four days. When I got back, I half expected to run into him skipping down the hallways of the hospital—or at least pacing up and down in front of his hospital room—but he was doing neither. I stopped at the nursing station to check where he was and how he was doing. The charge nurse answered my questions in a firm voice. "He hasn't eaten in two days," she said.

"Has he vomited?"

"No."

"Is he nauseated?"

"No."

"Well, sometimes that happens. More often the patients become nauseated and vomit, but not always. L-dopa can cause loss of appetite even without nausea," I explained.

She shook her head. "That's not it at all. He thinks we're trying to poison him."

"I know the food's not that good, but it's safe to eat."

"Dr. Klawans," she replied, ignoring my feeble attempt at humor, "he's in big trouble."

"What kind of trouble?"

"The day you left, he stopped eating his meals. We all figured it was just that he'd lost his appetite. He kept on taking his medicine, his L-dopa. And we could still see him walking incessantly up and down the hall. The L-dopa was obviously doing wonders for him. That night he paid one of the orderlies to pick up a pizza for him."

"To do what?"

"Get him a pizza. Lots of patients do things like that. The orderlies always check with us to make sure it's okay. After all, our food's not that good," she reminded me. "We let him do it. We were glad he felt like eating. Also, he'd been living in Tacoma for twenty-five years, and we were sure he couldn't get real pizza in Tacoma."

"So what happened?"

"The orderly also brought back a case of Cokes. Dr. Lipon ate only one slice of the pizza. The next day he stopped pacing up and down the hallway. He stayed in his room. Every few minutes he'd open the door, stick his head out, and look around and then go back in."

"All day long?" I asked.

"All day and all night."

"Why had he eaten only one piece of pizza?"

"He said it tasted funny."

"L-dopa can . . . ," I began.

"That's what we figured. We were wrong. He continued to take his pills, but no meals—none of our food. He accused the dietitian of trying to poison him. He takes his pills with the Cokes, which he guards twenty-four hours a day. I think he even uses the Coke to brush his teeth." She stopped. There was no reason to go on.

I had blown it. Dr. Lipon had gone from merely strange to overtly grandiose, and now to frankly paranoid. It was a progression I had seen before, but this time I had failed to recognize it at the grandiose stage and prevent further progression.

Why hadn't I seen it? Because he had included me in his grand scheme of things? Because it had flattered me? Or because he was a doctor and I'd given him the benefit of the doubt?

I went into his room. He wasn't there. I called his name three times. I was about to leave when the bathroom door opened a crack. "Are you alone?"

"Yes."

"Is it safe?"

"Safe?"

"Have they gotten to you, too?"

"Who?"

He laughed. It was not a normal laugh but a sinister one. "You know who."

"No one has gotten to me."

"Then why did you desert me and leave me at their mercy, alone, surrounded? They've been trying to poison me. But I'm smarter than any of them, than all of them. Than all of you."

"I didn't desert you," I said, trying desperately to think of some way to win back his confidence, to enter his mind on his side in this delusion. He had included me inside his grandiosity, and I had rejected that role. Was I now one of them and therefore an enemy to be totally excluded? Or was I still on his side?

"You left town."

"I had no choice."

"Were they after you, too? Were they trying to kill you?"

That was too extreme. "No."

"Then why did you leave me all alone?"

"The L-dopa." He was horrified. Was there something wrong with the L-dopa?

"I had to make sure the L-dopa was safe."

"I never. Oh, my God. Those Russian bastards. They got to the L-dopa. I knew I couldn't trust that chief nurse."

"Don't worry," I said. "The L-dopa is safe."

"We must save the world from them."

"Yes," I nodded. I was no longer one of them; I was on his side. It was them against us. "Tell me exactly what's happening."

For a moment he looked at me with a mixture of condescension and curiosity. Could I really not know? Could I be that naive?

"It's safe," I said.

He told me what had happened. The Russians had heard of our plan and were determined to stop us because, once we got to China and gave L-dopa to Mao, China would be our ally. That would spell the end for the Russians, so they were determined that we should never leave Chicago. They were trying to poison him. First the hospital food, then the water, then the pizza had been poisoned. And if the Russians could poison all of those things, they could get to the L-dopa and poison it.

"Is there anyone else we can trust?" I asked.

Once again I got the same look of incredulity. "No."

I had to figure out what to do next. In less than two weeks, I had transformed a normal man into a paranoid schizophrenic merely by giving him some L-dopa. "It's not safe," I said.

"What!"

"We can't trust any of them."

He nodded.

"They may have gotten to your L-dopa while I was gone. I will bring you some new L-dopa. I will give it to you myself, and you can take it as you need it."

"The L-dopa," he said. "They got to the L-dopa. We are done for. The Russians will win. That nurse, we must destroy her."

"No. I have a plan."

"A plan!" This interested him. Whenever the nurses brought him his medicine, he should not refuse the pills but take them and keep them in his room. He should then take the pills I gave him and keep the others for me so I could see what poison the Russians were using.

"And then we will go to China," he said.

"Yes," I agreed.

"And save the world."

"And save the world."

He followed my instructions to the letter. I brought him a bottle of pills. They were not L-dopa but a placebo made up to look exactly like the L-dopa. Three times a day, the nurses brought him L-dopa, and three times a day he took the pills I had left for him and collected their pills for me. Within two days, he was back pacing in the hallway. In three days he was slowly walking down the hall and eating his meals, complaining that the food did not taste right. In five days he looked exactly as he had the first time I had seen him: disabled by his Parkinson's disease, but no longer the man who would save the world if only the Russians didn't kill him first.

Dr. Lipon was right. The L-dopa was not safe. At least not for him.

His schizophrenia-like psychosis was caused by the L-dopa I gave him. The L-dopa entered his brain. Once there, it was converted to dopamine, and that dopamine triggered his psychosis. In a world that had long believed that behavior triggered behavior, that nurture caused psychiatric maladjustments to life, the role of the single rather obscure neurotransmitter in precipitating and maintaining a paranoid psychotic state was a major observation.

A schizophrenic form of psychosis-like parkinsonism is not a single disease entity. It is a symptom complex consisting of disturbances in thinking and feeling, including withdrawal, detachment from reality, disruption of interpersonal communication, and, often, hallucinations and delusions. The delusions are frequently grandiose or paranoid or a mixture of the two. Neither the underlying cause—what medical scientists like to call the pathogenesis—nor the way in which this cause produces the behavioral abnormalities—the pathophysiology— is completely understood. Unfortunately most of the literature about schizophrenia does not even separate these two very different processes. In basic terms the pathogenesis of schizophrenia consists of the primary defect, either genetic or environmental, while the pathophysiology consists of the manner in which this defect alters normal nerve cell or brain function, resulting in the abnormal behavior known as schizophrenia.

What happened to Dr. Lipon tells us nothing about the cause of schizophrenia, but it does tell us something about the way in which symptoms occur. Dopamine plays a role in that process.

After Dr. Lipon was discharged from the hospital, I learned that this had not been his first episode of acute paranoid psychosis. He had had two previous episodes. I learned this from a neurologist from Tacoma named Joe Ginsberg, who had been treating John for Parkinson's disease for several years. Ginsberg had tried to refer him to several places much nearer to Tacoma for L-dopa, but when he had told those neurologists about Dr. Lipon's psychiatric history, they had all refused to give him any L-dopa. They knew it wouldn't be safe. So Dr. Lipon came to me, without telling his own doctor, and he lied to me about his past history. Dr. Lipon's previous psychiatric episodes hadn't involved L-dopa, Mao, or the Russians but were similar paranoid delusions involving the Japanese and the Nazis. The L-dopa had merely reactivated the abnormal process that was already present inside his brain waiting to be triggered. The medication itself had not been the cause.

We don't know the cause or causes of schizophrenia. The fact that exposure to simple chemicals related to neurotransmitters can precipitate psychiatric episodes suggests that such chemicals might play a role in causing the disease. As a result of such reasoning, a great deal of the recent research in schizophrenia has been concerned primarily with finding a biochemical abnormality in patients with schizophrenia.

It is possible to think of schizophrenia as no different from any other form of behavior that results from the normal or abnormal function of brain cells. All behavior comes down to three basic steps. A small molecule (a neurotransmitter or a neurotransmitter-like drug) acts on a large molecule (receptor site) in order to produce a specific effect (excitatory or inhibitory) on the cell that contains that receptor. The sum of all the individual excitatory and inhibitory influences on a given nerve cell at any time will determine whether or not the neuron fires. The complex pattern of similar influences on a large number of neurons will determine the behavior of the organism. Alterations in any step of this process can participate in the production of abnormal behavior.

Neurotransmitter ⟶ Receptor Site ⟶ Behavior
(Small Molecule)   (Large Molecule)   (Environment)

All in all, the theories of the pathogenesis of schizophrenia fall into one of three broad categories, each of which involves a different mechanism. The first maintains that schizophrenia results from the action of some abnormal small molecule (a neurotransmitter or a psychotomimetic—psychosis-inducing—compound). The second suggests that schizophrenia involves an abnormal large molecule (a structural protein receptor or an enzyme). The third proposes that schizophrenia involves abnormal environmental influences that change the behavior caused by neurotransmitter-receptor interactions.

1. THE SMALL-MOLECULE HYPOTHESIS

Much of the biochemical research that supports the concept that one or more small molecules (neurotransmitter-like substance) cause schizophrenia is based on the model of drug-induced psychosis and focuses on finding an abnormal neurotransmitter-like molecule in schizophrenics. According to such theories, the individual himself either produces, or is exposed to, one or more of these psychotomimetic compounds and as a result becomes schizophrenic. Dr. Lipon was exposed to dopamine produced from L-dopa by his own brain and, as a result of the action of dopamine, experienced an episode of acute paranoid schizophrenia. In him a normally occurring small molecule caused psychosis. Could his other episodes have resulted from an analogous process?

This small-molecule hypothesis raises several questions. The most obvious are related to the actual existence of such compounds, their sites of action within the brain, and the mechanism by which they produce abnormal behavior in individuals who become schizophrenic. The small-molecule theories assume that the brains of schizophrenics are normal and that the schizophrenic is therefore, in a sense, poisoned by some abnormal molecule, a so-called psychotomimetic toxin. This could come about in a number of ways.

The abnormal molecule may be more potent at some specific receptor site than the normal neurotransmitter. The fact that all of the most effective drugs used in the treatment of schizophrenia are drugs that block specific dopamine receptor lends some weight to such a theory. Increased dopamine activity somewhere in Dr. Lipon's brain made him insane; removal of that dopamine resulted in resolution of his psychosis. In most other acute psychotic patients who have not been exposed to L-dopa, blocking dopamine receptors also helps to alleviate their psychosis.

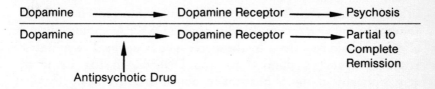

As far as we know, most patients with schizophrenia have never been exposed to significant amounts of L-dopa or any other abnormal small molecule. Dr. Lipon had not been so exposed in the past, but he had been psychotic twice before. The problem, of course, might not be the exposure to a foreign chemical, but the body's inability to resist exposure. We are all exposed to toxins every day, but our bodies are able to destroy (detoxify) them before they harm us. In patients who become schizophrenic, it is quite possible that the abnormal molecule is one that we are all exposed to but in the schizophrenic patient it is not detoxified at the normal rate, thus allowing it to act at the specific receptor site for a prolonged period.

The modern era of speculation about the possible role of small molecules in causing the schizophrenic psychoses began with the observation that most of the agents that cause hallucinations in humans are structurally similar to normal neuro-transmitters. Although the states produced by these agents do not really resemble schizophrenia, they are forms of psychosis. In 1962 Osmond and Smythies suggested that abnormal metabolites of epinephrine (adrenaline) might have a mescaline-like structure and effect and thus be responsible for schizophrenia. They suggested that 3, 4-dimethoxyphenyl-ethyla-mine (DMPEA), which looks very much like mescaline (the naturally occurring hallucinogen found in certain cacti and long used by Indians for its hallucinogenic effects), might be produced inside the brain by abnormal metabolism of adrenaline and might have psychotomimetic properties.

If DMPEA production within the body or brain itself is the primary abnormality in schizophrenia, then the DMPEA would be acting at normal receptor sites in the brain to elicit schizophrenia. If this were the case, then DMPEA should exist in the brains of patients with schizophrenia and not in the brains of normal individuals, and when administered to either schizophrenics or normal individuals, DMPEA should elicit a schizophrenic reaction. In the early 1960s several psychiatric research workers claimed to find DMPEA in the urine of schizophrenic patients but not in nonschizophrenics.

Imagine the excitement. The cause of schizophrenia was in our grasp:

DMPEA ⟶ Dopamine Receptor ⟶ Schizophrenia

But, alas, it was not true. Further research found that DMPEA given to either normal volunteers or schizophrenics in remission had no effect at all. Thus DMPEA does not produce schizophrenic symptoms and is not the cause of schizophrenia.

A similar and equally inconclusive argument has been made about the possible role of a variety of other small molecules in the production of schizophrenia. To prove that an abnormal small molecule acts on a normal brain to produce schizophrenia, such a molecule must be clearly demonstrated to be present in patients with schizophrenia but not in normal people, and to be able to elicit appropriate symptoms in both schizophrenics and normal subjects. Neither of the criteria has been met for any proposed psychotomimetic agent.

The best support for this type of theory is that, for the most part, our ability to treat the symptoms of schizophrenia consists of the various neuroleptics that block the ability of dopamine or dopamine-like false neurotransmitters from reaching dopamine receptors. These neuroleptic drugs are the treatment of choice in schizophrenia. They are more useful than the various types of psychotherapy, electroshock therapy, and placebos. Neuroleptics have been shown in controlled studies to significantly decrease thought disorder, blunted affect, withdrawal, autistic behavior mannerisms, hallucinations, uncooperativeness, and paranoid and grandiose behavior.

2. LARGE-MOLECULE HYPOTHESIS

Neuroleptics all block dopamine receptors. If the blockade of dopamine at the dopamine receptor sites is in fact the essential effect of such drugs in improving the symptoms of schizophrenia, then the pathophysiology of those symptoms might involve an abnormal dopamine-receptor site, an abnormal large molecule. The problem would not be exposure to some particular chemical or toxin or variability in the patient's ability to detoxify a common (or rare) toxin but in a different or abnormal response to a normal chemical due to some abnormal large molecule or receptor somewhere in the brain. According to such a line of reasoning, Dr. Lipon's psychosis was not caused by L-dopa becoming dopamine in his brain; the dopamine merely precipitated his psychosis because his brain itself contained abnormal cells that produced abnormal behavior when confronted with dopamine.

In this hypothesis, the problem is not in the chemical that enters the brain but in how the brain perceives and responds to that chemical.

There are some known differences in the ways in which schizophrenics and nonschizophrenics respond to certain chemicals or drugs. Chlorpromazine, the first known neuroleptic, produces a different effect in schizophrenics than in

normal individuals. Normal subjects on a lower dose show severe tremor and discomfort as well as marked effects on a
variety of psychological functions; schizophrenic subjects require 20 percent more of the drug before exhibiting significant
effects. These differences have to be related to a difference in
the response of either the receptor or the neurons upon which
chlorpromazine acts. One implication of these observations is
that the dopamine-receptor sites in the brains of schizophrenics may be abnormal.

3. THE ENVIRONMENTAL HYPOTHESIS

The influence of accumulated input derived from experience,
environmental stress, or emotional reinforcement must be an
essential component of schizophrenia. The one function that
clearly differentiates the brain and its cells from other organs
and their cells is the ability of brain cells to learn. The way in
which any previous behavior or experience influences future
behavior is the essence of learning. And since all behavior depends on neurotransmitter-receptor interactions, learning
must be intimately related to this process. A normal small
molecule can act as a normal receptor in the brain and still
result in an abnormal effect or behavior. The complex pathways and inputs beyond the initial receptor site can and do
modify the quality and nature of the effect generated by any
small molecule acting at its receptor site.

The effect of the hallucinogen mescaline, as it acts on normal receptor sites, depends greatly on what the brain has
learned before exposure to this chemical. Peyote, a mescaline
derivative, creates an acute religious state in Mexican Indians.
In other individuals in other settings, the response is significantly different. It is clear that the environment and experience of the individual largely determine the behavior produced
by psychotomimetic agents. In the same way, experience must
help to determine the behavioral response to normal neurotransmitters. If experience-related cellular functions are altered in a patient, the quality of drug-receptor interactions will
be distorted, regardless of the normal state of the individual
receptor sites and the small molecules.

What happened to John Lipon, M.D.? He did not save the world. He not even go to China. President Nixon did that. How much that improved the world is still not fully answered.

Dr. Lipon went back to Tacoma. A year later, when L-dopa was approved by the FDA for general use in the treatment of Parkinson's disease, his neurologist in Tacoma called me. Would it be safe to treat him?

Probably, I responded, with very low doses and very careful monitoring. The neurologist put him on 250 mg three times a day. Dr. Lipon's Parkinson's disease improved significantly—not as much as it had at larger doses, but he was able to function better. He was not able to go back to work or save the world, but he was more comfortable and less irascible, and he stayed just this side of grandiose and paranoid.

I have occasionally wondered about Dr. Lipon's view of world politics. Mao Tse-tung *did* have parkinsonism. Did it affect Mao's career? His decisions? The Cultural Revolution? Did the Gang of Four take advantage of a sick, disabled, slow, indecisive old man, or were they part of his paranoid response to the world mediated by the usual process?

Dopamine ⟶ Dopamine Receptor ⟶ Abnormal Behavior

None of us will ever know. I prefer to believe that the Cultural Revolution was not a manifestation of Mao's paranoia, but my experience with John Lipon and others like him has left the question open to speculation.

Author's Note

There are numerous discussions in the medical literature of dopamine on schizophrenia and L-dopa–induced psychosis. For a variety of reasons, I like the one I wrote with two of my students. While this article is a decade old, nothing published in the last ten years has significantly altered its general thrust:

Klawans, H. L., C. G. Goetz, and R. C. Westheimer. "The pharmacology of schizophrenia." *Clinical Neuropharmacology.* 1: 1–28 (1976).

5

Toscanini's Fumble

How is it that one fine morning Duchenne discovered a disease
that probably existed in the time of Hippocrates? . . . Why do we
perceive things so late, so poorly, with such difficulty? Why do
we have to go over the same set of symptoms twenty times
before we understand it? Why does the first statement of what
seems a new fact always leave us cold?
Because our minds have to take in something that deranges our
original set of ideas, but we are all of us like that in this
miserable world.
—J. M. Charcot (1872)

Michael Vernon had been admitted to the hospital because of
three brief episodes of dizziness, each lasting less than an
hour. During the first episode he also had double vision, while
during the second his left arm and left leg were weak. During
the third episode his right arm and leg had been weak. After
the third episode Mr. Vernon called his internist, who immediately admitted him to the hospital and asked me to see him in
consultation.

As a full-time academic physician in a medical school, I come
accompanied by an entourage and preceded by individual parts
of that group. By the time I saw Mr. Vernon, he'd already been
examined by a medical student, who was spending a month
studying neurology with me, and by a first-year neurology
resident.

Michael Vernon was seventy-one years old and, according to
what he'd told the student and the resident, had been in excellent health until the first of the three episodes of dizziness hit
him just two weeks earlier. None of Mr. Vernon's episodes had
lasted as much as fifteen minutes, and when they were over, he
felt back to normal.

73

But worried. When the first episode started, he was worried that he was about to have a stroke. He'd had friends whose strokes left them paralyzed on one side, with difficulty speaking, or worse. He waited in fear, and when the episode passed, he was relieved beyond belief. He had not gotten weak in either arm or leg, and his speech was normal. Perhaps, he hoped, if he ignored it, it would never come back.

But it did come back. After the second episode, his left arm and leg did get weak. However, the dizziness and weakness went away again, so he did nothing about it. Once again, he hoped that his symptoms would never return. They did, and he could not ignore that third episode because his son was with him, saw what happened, and insisted that he call his doctor.

It was the medical student, a bright fourth-year student named Jill Coan, who gave me all of this information. She'd taken a thorough history and examined the patient completely. The patient's neurological examination was entirely normal. The resident, Irv Noren, confirmed the history and the physical.

I asked the student if she had made a diagnosis.

She had. "Transient ischemic attack, or TIA," she replied, using one of the many acronyms so beloved to all young physicians.

"What's that mean in English?"

"Well, for some reason, for a few seconds Mr. Vernon wasn't getting enough blood up to his brain. It wasn't bad enough or didn't last long enough to cause a stroke, but it was severe enough so that part of his brain didn't work right for a while."

It was the type of answer I hoped to get from a bright medical student, complete with the acronym. Today I expect medical students to be able to make that diagnosis correctly and to understand the entire process. Yet no medical student could possibly have given that answer just two generations ago. Whatever had happened to Mr. Vernon had undoubtedly been happening to patients for centuries, if not millennia; yet before the 1950s, even experienced neurologists were unable to make such a diagnosis. At that time no one had fully conceptualized the process.

Most strokes occur when a region of the brain is deprived of its blood supply long enough for the nerve cells or pathways in that area to become injured. If that occurs in an area that controls movement, the patient becomes weak. If it involves an area that controls speech, the victim becomes unable to speak (aphasic), and so forth. As soon as the flow of blood containing the needed oxygen and nutrients is interrupted, the neurons stop functioning and the clinical signs and symptoms start. But the death of the nerve cells doesn't occur quite that soon. They can survive for some period of time, minutes at least, with an interrupted blood supply. If the interruption goes on too long, they die, but if the blood flow is restored before irreversible damage or death occurs, they recover. They return to normal function, and so does the patient.

The medical word for lack of blood supply is *ischemia*. Hence such a reversible episode is a TIA, or transient ischemic attack.

Michael Vernon had had three TIAs. Three times the blood supply to one or more crucial regions of his brain had become insufficient. All three times it had been temporary and he'd recovered. But that still left unanswered questions. So I asked my entourage: Why did he have TIAs? Why those particular TIAs, and why at those particular times?

Neither the student nor the resident could tell me the answers to those questions, so the three of us went to see Mr. Vernon. He gave me much the same story he'd already told Jill Coan and Irv Noren. I examined him. His examination was not merely normal; it was remarkable. He looked far younger than his age. He was vigorous and without an ounce of fat, obviously a man who took care of his body.

"Do you exercise?" I asked, although the answer was obvious.

He did. He'd been a runner in college and said he'd never stopped running.

Had he been running when the attacks occurred?

No, he hadn't.

What had he been doing?

He knew precisely. During the first attack, he'd been chopping some logs. During the second, he'd been shoveling snow off his driveway. The third had started during an exercise routine.

"Jumping jacks?" I suggested.

He thought for a moment and then agreed. "Jumping jacks."

I felt his pulses again. This time I felt both wrists at the same time. The pulse on the right was ever so slightly weaker than the one on the left, and each individual pulsation was more prolonged. It lasted slightly longer than its counterpart on the right. The difference was so slight that it was indistinguishable if you felt the pulses one at a time; you had to check both simultaneously.

I had my answer; I knew why Michael Vernon had had his three TIAs.

Now I had to do three things: I had to teach Jill and Irv about the process. I also had to teach Mr. Vernon, since his education was a necessary step in preventing any further TIAs. Then I had to prove that I was right.

I did something I rarely do. I opted to combine the first two steps as much as possible. I explained the concept of TIAs to Mr. Vernon as clearly as I could. He grasped it immediately. He was a chemical engineer, and even though he had officially retired at age 68, he was still an active consultant.

He also grasped the unasked and unanswered questions. Why had he had those three TIAs? Did they mean he would go on to have a stroke? If so, was there anything we could do to change the odds?

I turned to Jill. "What's Mr. Vernon's blood pressure?" I asked.

"One twenty-eight over eighty-two," she replied. That was normal.

"Which arm?" I asked her.

This time she did not have the answer on the tip of her tongue. She thought for a moment. "Left arm."

"What was his blood pressure in his other arm?"

She didn't know.

"Would it be important to know his blood pressure in both arms?"

"I guess so," she said without much conviction. In her young career, taking the blood pressure in both arms had never helped her understand a patient or his disease any better.

"Did you ever hear of Bernoulli's principle?"

Jill had no idea what I was asking her about, nor did Irv Noren. They had both studied Bernoulli's principle in college physics, but it obviously had not made much of an impression on either of them.

It had on Michael Vernon. "Bernoulli was Swiss," he began. I had always assumed, incorrectly I now learned, that Bernoulli had been Italian. I said as much.

Mr. Vernon assured me he was Swiss, although undoubtedly from the part of Switzerland that borders on Italy. He also told me Bernoulli's entire history. Daniel Bernoulli, of Bernoulli's principle fame, was from a family of famous mathematicians. He lived from 1700 until 1782. His principle explains why airplanes fly. According to Bernoulli's principle, pressure is inversely proportional to velocity; the greater the velocity, the lower the pressure. An airplane's wings are convex, and the air that goes over the top must travel over this convexity, so it must go farther than the air that goes straight under the wing. If it goes farther in the same time, its speed or, more correctly, its velocity, must be greater than the velocity of the air passing under the wing. As a result, the downward pressure on the wing will be less than the upward pressure exerted by the slower air passing below the wing. So the plane flies. "Pressure," Mr. Vernon repeated, "is inversely proportional to velocity."

Clearly I was not the only teacher in the room. It was time to shift gears. "What do you know about the blood supply to the back of the brain, Jill?"

"There are two vertebral arteries. One comes up each side of the neck, and then they combine to form the basilar artery."

My teaching was now aimed at both the medical and the nonmedical people in the room. "The basilar artery formed by the two vertebral arteries supplies blood to the brain stem, the part of the brain that connects the two hemispheres to the spinal cord. The brain stem carries out several unique functions. One of these is the coordination of eye movement. Lack of this coordination causes double vision. It is the only part of the brain that controls movement of both sides of the body. So if a patient has TIAs in which he has double vision and alternating weakness, first one side of the body, then the other . . . ," I hesitated.

Mr. Vernon jumped into the breach. He would have made an excellent medical student. "Then the TIAs are due to some problem in the vertebral or basilar arteries."

"Correct. Now we know that the blood comes up each side of the neck in the two vertebral arteries to enter the one basilar artery. The next question is, what is the source of the vertebral arteries?"

"The subclavian arteries—just before they go into the arms," Irv replied.

"Good. Now what happens to the blood flow to the arm when you exercise?"

I looked at Mr. Vernon, hoping that he could once again supply the answer. "It must increase to meet the metabolic needs of the muscles."

"Correct. What if you exercise the arm, and the subclavian artery is partially blocked? In that case the blood supply still increases by increasing in velocity. And what does that do to the pressure in the subclavian artery, Jill?"

"According to Bernoulli's principle, the pressure should go down as the velocity goes up."

"And since blood flows from high pressure to low pressure, what will happen in the vertebral arteries?" This time I answered my own question. "The blood will go up the one vertebral artery that has normal pressure to the point where it meets the opposite vertebral artery. The pressure in that artery which is the one coming from the partially blocked subclavian—the artery with increased velocity and therefore decreased pressure—is of course lower. Blood flows from higher pressure to lower. Hence the blood goes up one vertebral artery and then down the other into the subclavian artery where the pressure is low. That's why this is called a *subclavian steal syndrome*. The subclavian artery in essence steals the blood from the brain, and as a result the patient has a TIA." All three of the students understood the mechanism behind the subclavian steal syndrome.

"Is that what happened to me?" Michael Vernon asked. Naturally, the specific was of more interest to him than the general.

"I think so."

"Why?"

"You had the right precipitating factors—arm exercise—all three times. And all three times, you stopped exercising and the attacks went away. And your pulse on the right is weaker and more prolonged than the one on the left."

"Can you prove it?"

"If your blood pressure is less in your right arm. Quick, Jill, the cuff."

She took her blood-pressure cuff out of her black bag and began to take Mr. Vernon's blood pressure—in both arms. That gave me a few minutes to do some more teaching.

"What single TIA—subclavian steal—was observed by more people than any other TIA in the history of the world? Perhaps ten million and more, and no one knew what it was?"

All three of them looked at me with expressions that varied from blank to openly puzzled. "Think a bit. In what occupation would subclavian steals be an occupational hazard?" There was no reply. "Anything in which the patient suddenly uses his arms vigorously and repetitively?"

"Carpentry," Irv suggested.

"No, I've never heard of ten million people observing a carpenter at the same time. Something that's very vigorous, involves the arm, and you do only part of the time?"

No one ventured a guess.

"I'll give you a hint. It has to do with music."

"Playing a violin?" Mr. Vernon guessed.

"Close, but no cigar."

"Conducting!" Jill said.

"Right. Now who was the most famous conductor of the first half of the twentieth century?"

Silence.

"You medical students and residents are getting too young. Think. Before 1955, and not Xavier Cugat."

"Toscanini, Arturo Toscanini," answered Mr. Vernon.

"Correct, and he was a vigorous conductor—not exactly a Bernstein, but far from Fritz Reiner. And do you know what happened during his last broadcast with the NBC Symphony Orchestra? He was conducting Wagner. All of a sudden it was obvious that something was wrong. He had lost control of the orchestra briefly. The music was suddenly replaced by twenty or thirty seconds of silence, and then they cut in with a recording of Brahms's First Symphony. The irony of it—to replace Toscanini's Wagner with Brahms—and with Walter conducting. In about two minutes Toscanini was back conducting. Later the papers said that the maestro had stumbled and dropped his baton and then recovered. Based on what you know now, what do you think happened to the maestro?"

"From your description, it sounds like he had a TIA," Mr. Vernon replied.

"Why did he have it?"

"I suppose the vigorous movement of his arms caused a subclavian steal, and then he recovered," our patient continued.

"That's also my guess. But 1954 was several years before the subclavian steal syndrome had been described. No one had ever heard of it in 1954, so of course no one diagnosed it in Toscanini."

It was time to get back to Mr. Vernon's own problem. "One twenty-five over eighty on the left," Jill said. "Ninety over sixty on the right."

"I rest my case."

"What does it mean to me, Dr. Klawans?" asked the patient. Someone had finally asked the key question.

TIAs, I explained, were usually a warning sign for a possible stroke. *But*, and that but was a big but, it all depended upon the cause of the TIAs. His TIAs were due to a subclavian steal syndrome, and very few people with subclavian steals went on to have strokes. If he stopped the kinds of exercise that caused his TIAs, they too would go away.

We discussed the other therapeutic options. There were two. The first was surgery on the partially obstructed subclavian artery. The artery was narrowed by atherosclerosis, and such clogged arteries could be cleaned out. Why not his? Then he could exercise all he wanted to. However, I thought surgery was too risky. It was a major procedure. The chances of complications—the morbidity (serious illness such as strokes) and the mortality (death)—due to the procedure were far greater than his risk of a stroke.

The same was true for the use of drugs known as anticoagulants, so-called blood thinners. Their long-term use in patients at any age carried significant risks of morbidity and mortality from abnormal bleeding. At his age that risk increased and was far greater than the threat of his disease.

Thus, I thought both options were far too dangerous. After all, Mr. Vernon's chances of having a stroke were small. He was satisfied, and the consultation was over.

His internist wasn't satisfied, however. There had to be something we could do other than tell him not to do whatever it was that caused his symptoms. His own wife could have told him that much. The internist arranged for a vascular surgeon to see Mr. Vernon in consultation. The surgeon, Anthony Mele, agreed with the diagnosis but wanted to do an angiogram to outline the arteries and actually see the obstruction and then to operate on it.

When I saw Mr. Vernon the next day, he told me of Dr. Mele's opinion. I repeated my previous opinions. "If Toscanini had changed his style, could he have gone on conducting?" he asked.

"Yes."

"For how long?"

"Until he died."

"Of a stroke."

"No, of whatever he died from, but not a stroke. Toscanini did not die of a stroke."

Michael Vernon did not undergo an angiogram. He had no interest in having the surgery, so the angiogram was superfluous. Anticoagulation was equally out of the question as far as he was concerned.

I went to see him the morning he was to be discharged. We talked of many things. He needed to be reassured that he had made the right decision. I did the best I could, but time would be the best reassurance. When he had no more TIAs, he would gain confidence that he would not have a stroke.

We also talked about Toscanini. We were both interested in classical music. I complained that I could no longer call my Toscanini story the "Italian Connection." I had used that title since I had thought Bernoulli, Toscanini, and the first man who ever demonstrated reversal of flow in the vertebral artery, a radiologist named Contormi, were all Italian. But now it turned out that Bernoulli was Swiss, not Italian.

Mr. Vernon smiled. He told me I could still call it the Italian Connection. Bernoulli's principle, he assured me, is a general law of physics that applies under a wide variety of conditions, including the flight of airplanes. When it is applied to fluids in constricted pipes such as his own subclavian artery, it is often called the Venturi effect. It was Venturi who first applied Bernoulli's principle to constricted channels of fluid flow within pipes—and Venturi was an Italian. Besides, Bernoulli was a Swiss of Italian descent.

I originally saw Michael Vernon in 1978. He writes me every year on my birthday. (How he found out when my birthday is I have no idea.) He signs the cards Mickey, so I now call him Mickey. He is still alive and well. He has not had a stroke, and he's had no further TIAs.

Each year the card is accompanied by some classical records, usually the latest Chicago Symphony Orchestra records—Mahler with Solti or Levine, or Bruckner with Barenboim. But this year it was not records, it was CDs. And not the CSO, but the NBC Symphony Orchestra led by Arturo Toscanini. Beethoven's Seventh, the unrivaled 1937 recording.

"Too bad," his note read, "that the steal syndrome had not been invented when Toscanini had his. Had it been, there might be even more great records to be transferred to CDs. As soon as the Verdi Requiem is released, I will send it to you. Mickey."

Toscanini conducted his last concert in 1954. I was still in high school at the time, and I remember listening to it with my mother and father. Looking back, I like to think that I really wanted to listen to it, but I probably didn't. I was sixteen years old, and my heroes were Chico Carrasquel, Nellie Fox, and Minnie Minoso—not Arturo Toscanini, Bruno Walter, or Lennie Bernstein, although Bernstein was beginning to come up quickly on the outside.

We had gotten our first television in 1951. Actually it was a family entertainment center—TV, AM-FM radio, and phonograph all together in some overpriced piece of blond furniture. The wood matched the rest of the pieces in our living room. As a result of this purchase, tough decisions had to be made, not just which channel to watch, but whether to watch TV or listen to the radio (people still listened to radio then, not just as a solitary experience while driving a car or background while doing something else, but as real entertainment), or listen to records. "Davy Crockett" versus *La Traviata*.

At times, it seemed that most of the family entertainment took the form of arguments. Each Saturday afternoon, my mother and I had the same battle—the Metropolitan Opera versus college football. I was not the one who battled on the side of the Met. To me, 260-pound linemen were magnificent athletes, while 260-pound sopranos were an obscenity. And they screeched too much.

The Toscanini–NBC Symphony broadcasts were only on radio. There were no TV-FM simulcasts back then, no stereo broadcasts at all. It was on a Saturday afternoon but late, after whatever sports event I might have wanted to watch was long over, but it wouldn't have mattered if it wasn't over. For in our household Toscanini took precedence over everything. I dread to think what would have happened if a Toscanini concert had been broadcast during a White Sox World Series game. Fortunately, the Sox never made the World Series during Toscanini's lifetime.

My parents, of course, listened to that concert in 1954 on the living room radio, so I couldn't watch TV. I was expected to listen with them, and I understood why: not because he was the greatest living conductor, but because he was Toscanini. Toscanini had refused to conduct in Salzburg after the Anschluss. He had never conducted in Nazi Germany, he had publicly rebuked Hitler, and he had never performed in his native Italy once the Fascists, led by Benito Mussolini, seized power. This was a man whose principles I had been raised to admire, and admire them I did.

The concert began. Toscanini, conducting as vigorously as ever, had a TIA. He recovered and finished the concert—never to conduct again. No one told him he had had a subclavian steal syndrome and all he had to do was move his arms less. No one knew.

It wasn't until seven years later that the disease was really recognized. In 1961 Reivich, Holling, Robert, and Toole described two patients with TIAs related to partial obstruction of the left subclavian artery that produced reversal of blood flow in the left vertebral artery. The blood went up the right vertebral artery and then, instead of going up into the basilar artery to supply the brain stem, went down the left vertebral artery and into the left arm.

I read that article for the first time in 1962. I immediately knew what had happened to Toscanini. But Toscanini had died in 1957, three years after his TIA and four years before the report of Reivich and his colleagues.

I had learned something very important nevertheless. There are patients we see with diseases that we cannot diagnose, not because they are rare, or difficult to diagnose, but because no one else had yet been smart enough to realize that they are new, different diseases. It's difficult to diagnose diseases that have not been described.

Before 1950 there was no such thing as TIAs. They were all called something else. Before 1961 there were no such things as subclavian steal syndromes. They were there, of course, but physicians did not know enough to recognize them. Now we do. And God only knows what diagnoses we will discover in the next ten years.

That's why I tell the Toscanini story to medical students— not because they should know about subclavian steals. They should, but subclavian steals are rare, and that knowledge will have little effect on them or their patients. But understanding one limitation, a limitation that patients must also accept, might help make my students better and more understanding physicians. A physician can only be expected to diagnose diseases that other physicians have already diagnosed. Physicians are still discovering new diseases, as the subclavian steal syndrome was discovered in 1961.

Usually such a discovery requires a great degree of clinical acumen and good luck. The right mind must be at the right place to see the right patients. Such physicians are rare, and most of us recognize the uniqueness of their abilities. That's probably why we tend to honor them by attaching their names to what they have described.

Author's Note

James Toole, for many years the chairman of the Department of Neurology at Bowman Gray School of Medicine in Winston Salem, North Carolina, played a pivotal role in the recognition of the subclavian steal syndrome and the part that reversal of blood flow in the vertebral artery played in this disorder. He was a coauthor of the first complete description:

Reivich, M., E. Holling, B. Roberts, and J. F. Toole. "Reversal of blood flow through the vertebral artery and its effect on cerebral arculation." *New England Journal of Medicine.* 263: 878–85 (1961).

He also helped to prove that exercise of the appropriate upper extremity (the Toscanini/Venturi effect) causes reversal of flow in a vertebral artery:

Sammartini, W. F., and J. F. Toole. "Reversed vertebral artery flow: the effect of limb exercise." *Archives of Neurology* 10: 590–94 (1964).

He confirmed the existence of this new disease in a 1964 editorial in *Annals of Internal Medicine* (61: 159–62), "Reversed Vertebral Artery Flow and Cerebral Vascular Insufficiency."

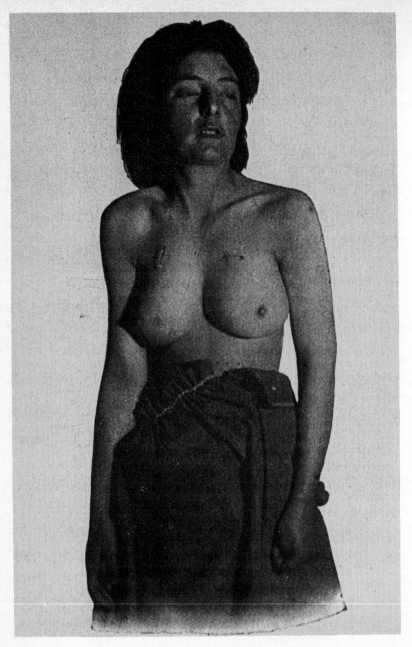

Universal anesthesia in a hysterical patient. Sterilized safety-pins have
been pushed through the skin on both sides without producing bleeding.
Hysterical contracture of the left hand is also present.

6

The Eye of the Beholder

His mouth is almost constantly opening and shutting as if he
were chewing. He has a strange method of frequently twirling
his fingers and twisting his hands. His body is in a continual
agitation seesawing up and down; his feet are never a moment
quiet; and in short his whole person is in perpetual motion.
F. Burney, *The Diary of Fanny Burney*

'Pray, Dr. Johnson, why do you make such strange gestures?'
'From bad habit,' [he replied]. 'Do you, my dear, take care to
guard against bad habits.'
J. Boswell, *Life of Johnson*

Had Johnson lived at a later date science would have been able,
if not to cure his oddities, at least to name them.
Christopher Hollis, *Dr. Johnson*

I've never been able to discover her name. No one knows it.
Her picture has hung in my office ever since I finished my
residency and had an office I could call my own. Not because I
like to hang pictures of half-clothed, or half-unclothed, women
in my office. Not because I have a thing for women with large
breasts. Or for large breasts with safety pins stuck through
them. Far from it. Sadomasochism is not one of my hobbies.

Her picture is there to remind me of my limitations as a
physician and observer. Not only is it true that we can diagnose
only those diseases that others have already described; we can
see only those things that others have seen and understood.

Nothing typifies this insoluble problem better than the medical history of Dr. Samuel Johnson (1709–1784). Johnson was
acknowledged during his lifetime as the greatest man of his
era, and this acknowledgment continues to this day. He is the
only English literary figure whose name is attached to the time
in which he lived—the Age of Johnson. Not even Shakespeare
has received this honor; that great playwright lived and wrote
in the Elizabethan Age. A respected poet, playwright, and bi-

ographer, Johnson edited the greatest of all the folios of the works of Shakespeare, and he singlehandedly produced the first great dictionary of the English language.

Throughout his entire life, Johnson manifested tics, jerks, habitual spasms, gesticulations, articulations, mannerisms, motor habits, and more. To his compatriots, these movements were considered merely the peculiarities of this man of genius. Johnson died in 1784 without benefit of a diagnosis. One hundred and one years later, Gilles de la Tourette described the disease that bears his name, Tourette's syndrome, and that Samuel Johnson undoubtedly manifested. Today I make that diagnosis at least once each week. Before 1885 it did not exist as a disease, merely as something that people had without knowing what they had.

The nameless woman with safety pins in her breasts was diagnosed as having hysteria. Hysteria is a disorder in which the patient develops specific neurological symptoms, such as paralysis or weakness, for reasons that are entirely psychological.

Why? For one reason it was the age of hysteria; hysteria was in the air. It was common, much more common than it is today, and no one knows why. So common that the brilliant minds of the day studied it—Jean-Martin Charcot, the world's first professor of neurology, as well as Freud, and many others.

The photograph of the nameless woman dates from 1893. Breuer and Freud's *Five Case Studies in Hysteria*, neurologist Freud's first venture into psychiatry, was published two years later in 1895 and began a new epoch.

And why was she diagnosed as being hysterical? It was the pins. She didn't feel them. She felt no pain in her breasts or other areas of her chest; yet she felt touch—a case that gave those who were studying either sadomasochism or hysteria a field day. It was also the era of Krafft-Ebbing, who documented the wide range of human sexual perversions.

But, of course, such a diagnosis was based on one simple assumption: Loss of the ability to sense pain without loss of the ability to sense touch could not be due to a disease of the nervous system and hence was hysterical. And that assumption, we now know, was wrong.

In the nerves that go from the spinal cord to the skin, pain and touch travel together; you can't lose one without the other. But once these nerve fibers enter the spinal cord, that is no longer true. The fibers carrying pain and temperature cross to the other side immediately, while those conveying touch linger a while, staying on the same side before meandering slowly across to the other side of the cord and brain. Something wrong in the center of the cord could cut the crossing fibers carrying pain and temperature and spare those transmitting touch.

Is there any disease that does that? There is one and, for all practical purposes, only one: a cyst of the spinal cord. These cysts are now called *syringomyelia*, or tube of the cord. And dissociated sensory loss—loss of pain and temperature with preservation of touch—is the classic manifestation of a tubular cyst, or syrinx, within the spinal cord.

Purvis-Stuart, the English neurologist who examined this woman, called her hysterical. He did not know about dissociated sensory loss. But he should have known she was not hysterical.

Look closely at the picture. Her left arm and hand are smaller than their counterparts on the right. This loss of muscle mass or atrophy was said to be part of her hysteria.

Look more closely. Her left arm is shorter than her right arm. While it is perhaps conceivable that hysteria and disuse could cause some loss of muscle mass, it could not make the bones get shorter. Hysteria is out as a sole diagnosis. But what about syringomyelia?

How could a syrinx make one arm shorter? A syrinx commonly gets both the crossing fibers for pain and temperature and also invades the motor cells of the cord, but only on one side. It squeezes those cells out and kills them, and the muscles, in turn, atrophy. If this process starts before growth is complete, the atrophy inhibits growth of that arm. Her left arm did not shrink, it just never grew fully.

Syringomyelia is the only disease that causes both unilateral atrophy and failure of growth and dissociated sensory loss. And, like Tourette's syndrome, it is a disease that I observe and diagnose today because I know about it.

But what illnesses do we still miss because no one has yet described them? Only time will tell.

AUTHOR'S NOTE

Samuel Johnson's abnormal movements have been analyzed in two related publications:

Murray, T. J. "Dr. Samuel Johnson's abnormal movements." *Gilles de las Tourette's Syndrome*, ed. A. J. Friedhoff and T. M. Chase, 25–30. New York: Raven Press, 1982.

Murray, T. J. "Dr. Samuel Johnson's movement disorders." *British Medical Journal* 1: 1610–14 (1979).

As late as 1948, before the recent rebirth of interest in Tourette's syndrome, the eminent British neurologist Lord Russell Brain believed that Johnson's tics were psychogenic, since he could suppress them at times:

Brain, W. R. "Some reflections on genius." *Lancet* 1: 661–65 (1948).

This suppressibility is now believed to be a characteristic of Tourette's syndrome. To see how thinking on the same disease can evolve over a period of thirty years, compare these papers to McHenry's 1967 discussion:

McHenry, L. C. "Samuel Johnson's tics and gesticulation." *Journal of the History of Medicine and Allied Sciences* 22: 152–168 (1967).

For the interested reader, Tourette's original description has finally been translated into English:

Goetz, C. G., and H. L. Klawans. "Gilles de la Tourette on Tourette syndrome." *Gilles de las Tourette's Syndrome*, ed. A. J. Friedhoff and T. M. Chase, 1–18. New York: Raven Press, 1982.

In his paper, Tourette clearly emphasized that tics are an entirely separate class of abnormal movements that must be differentiated from chorea in part on the basis of the character of the movements and in part on the basis of postural attitudes seen in choreatic disorders and not in patients with tics. This was a major advance in the classification of abnormal movements and movement disorders.

Tourette also insisted that this disorder was a neurological movement disorder and not a form of insanity or psychiatric disorder. This concept was unfortunately ignored until all too recently. His definition of this disorder as a lifelong illness consisting primarily of multiple tics, habits, spasms, and vocalizations, which was based on diagnoses made during the patients' adulthood, is still accepted. However, the relationship between adult Tourette's and multiple tics of childhood, a disorder not recognized by Tourette, remains unclear. The latter may be but a variant of full-blown Tourette's syndrome.

7

Spontaneous Generation

I have drawn your attention to this form of chorea, gentlemen,
not that I considered it of any great practical importance to you,
but merely as a medical curiosity, and as such it may have some
interest.
—George Huntington (1872)

Mrs. Morton Cooper was about fifty-three years old when I
first met her. She was a handsome woman, and I don't mean
that as an insult. She was tall, her posture erect, and her figure
still full and attractive. I doubt if she had gained a single pound
in her adult life. Her hair was just beginning to turn gray—salt
and pepper would describe it. When she was twenty-five I'm
sure she was considered to be beautiful.

Usually when I meet people in my office I know their exact
ages, but she was not the patient, so the best I could do was
observe her and make an educated guess. I hate guessing, although I am a rather good guesser—observation and estimates
based on observation are part and parcel of my job as a neurologist. I guessed her to be in her early fifties.

From her demeanor, it was apparent that she was no longer
interested in being beautiful. She had brought her son Walter
into my office for a neurological evaluation, for a second opinion. It was not just any second opinion that she wanted, but
mine. I had come highly recommended, for I was then Secre-
tary-General of the World Federation of Neurology's Research
Group on Huntington's Chorea. The title is far more impres-

93

sive than the job description, but it certainly implied that I have more experience with Huntington's chorea than most neurologists. And I do—far more.

She would get the opinion she had come for, but it was not the opinion she wanted. It was merely the truth. A painful truth which I already knew as I watched her son part shuffle, part lurch, and part dance into my office.

Her son had Huntington's chorea, or Huntington's disease, as it is now called in this country. I would thus confirm her worst fears and enter into a test of wills over an entirely different issue, the question of spontaneous generation. She not only chose the area of conflict, she also picked out what to call it.

The term *spontaneous generation* to me had always meant the medieval argument about whether maggots appeared spontaneously in putrid meat or instead required other organisms to produce them. It was as intellectually sterile an argument as the contemporary discussions about the seat of the soul or angels on the head of a pin. The debate had finally been put to rest by that genius of nineteenth-century science and scientific method, Louis Pasteur. No one today argues about spontaneous generation.

No one except this woman. But here the issue was not the spontaneous appearance of maggots on decaying meat but the not-so-spontaneous mutation within a sperm which then delivered the unwanted gene to her womb. That sperm united with a single egg and developed into a son, a son who was now twenty-eight years old and had Huntington's chorea.

The son was the second of Mrs. Cooper's four children. The oldest was a daughter, alive and well at age thirty with three small children of her own. There was another daughter who was twenty-four and unmarried and a son aged twenty-one, single and in college.

And her twenty-eight-year-old son Walter, the patient. Chief complaint: nervousness.

His story was one I had heard far too often. Slowly, subtly, neither he nor his family was sure when or how, his behavior had changed. It had begun three, perhaps four, years earlier.

He had always been a bit high-strung, easily excited, but that
had been getting worse and worse. He'd fly off the handle for
no reason. He couldn't concentrate, and his memory was not
what it had been. He had been a high school English teacher
but had lost that job two years ago. He now worked as a jani-
tor. He had been unable to read a book for two years. He
sometimes got lost now in the middle of TV shows, confusing
the characters, forgetting the plot. All he watched now were
reruns of children's shows like "Leave It to Beaver."

I listened and watched as he talked. His body was never still.
His muscles jerked continuously, first one, then another. Each
jerk caused a movement—brief, sudden, purposeless. His right
arm. His left shoulder. His jaw. The right arm again but in a
different direction.

Jerks. Twitches. First one way, then another. Random, serv-
ing no useful purpose.

Sometimes he would try to mask the movements, to inte-
grate them into something that we might call normal activity.
A severe upward twitch of his right arm resulted in an attempt
to smooth down his hair. When his left leg jerked out, he
swung it over so that he was sitting cross-legged. The movements went on and on.

They were the movements of chorea. The word *chorea* comes
from the Greek word for dance, like the better-known word
choreography, and Walter also had progressive loss of intellectual
function. This we call *dementia*. It was a formula I had know for
years:

Chorea + Dementia = Huntington's Chorea

It was a diagnosis that could be supported by seeing a particular pattern of atrophy of the brain on a CAT scan. I looked at
the chart. The CAT scan, already done, showed the type of
atrophy usually seen in Huntington's chorea.

It was not proof positive, however. Only a family history
was proof positive, for Huntington's is invariably hereditary.

It is inherited as a dominant gene. If a parent has the disease,
then each child of that parent has a fifty-fifty chance of developing the disease. But there are no carriers; if a person does
not inherit the disease from his parent, then he cannot pass it

on to his own children. Conversely, if a person has the disease, then one of his parents has to have had it as well.

This young man had Huntington's chorea. Ergo either his father or his mother had the disease.

I collected the necessary data from the patient's mother. Her father died at age seventy-seven of a heart attack with no evidence of neurological disease. Her mother was eighty-three and had no neurological disease. Nor did anyone else in her family.

Mrs. Cooper's husband therefore had to be the progenitor. He had to have had Huntington's. He had died at age forty-three, she said. My ears pricked up. Many Huntington's patients die in their forties. He had died in a hunting accident, she said.

It was not what I had expected to hear. He had had no neurological problems—no jerks, twitches, personality changes, depression, dementia, or memory loss. Nothing. I pushed as hard as I could, trying to find something on which to hang my hat. I couldn't.

He had died in an accident.

Sudden death is common in Huntington's chorea: sudden choking; death in a fire, like Woody Guthrie's mother; suicide. But those patients were rarely normal before death. His father was.

I was suspicious. No, it was more than that—I was downright skeptical.

But accidents do happen, even in families with Huntington's chorea. Besides, if the father had had Huntington's, he had to have inherited it from someone, and his parents were free of any taint of disease. And all four of his grandparents were equally free of any taint.

End of the line. No family history. No final diagnosis.

But I knew Walter had Huntington's chorea. And I told them that that was my best diagnosis. I couldn't prove it, but they had come to me for an opinion, and that was my opinion. That's how the first visit ended.

Two days later I got a call from Mrs. Cooper. She had been reading about Huntington's disease and had a question to ask me. If her husband had Huntington's, was it true that each of the other children had a fifty-fifty chance of getting the disease?

Yes.

And those who got it could give it to their children?

Yes.

I did not see her again for several months and did not give the matter much more thought. I see a large number of patients with Huntington's chorea, probably as many as any other neurologist in the country. One more patient does not cause me to reflect much.

I have spent a great deal of the last twenty years of my life studying Huntington's chorea. When you have done that, one patient more or less rarely affects your understanding of a disease or its impact on its victims or other family members. But Mrs. Cooper was to affect mine.

Huntington's chorea has a significance that transcends its relative infrequency as a disease; neither its historical nor its scientific importance should be underrated. It was one of the pivotal clinical studies of a new disease that, in the years following the Civil War, suddenly gained international stature for American medicine. It was the first disease to be named after an American physician.

George Huntington (1850–1916) was born in East Hampton, Long Island. His family already had been in America for over 200 years, and the Huntingtons traced their descent from Simon Huntington of Norwich, England, who with his wife Margaret Baret and children sailed to America in 1633. In 1797 Dr. Abel Huntington (our Dr. Huntington's grandfather) settled in East Hampton, Long Island, and soon became the leading physician in the region. He was well known as the first physician on Long Island to remove a kidney stone from a patient's bladder, a heroic undertaking in that era.

Abel Huntington was no less prominent. He had been one of the first American physicians to take advantage of Jenner's discovery that cowpox vaccination prevented smallpox. He personally prepared and preserved cowpox virus for vaccination and was in charge of a retreat for those who had been inoculated. Active in civic affairs as well as medical affairs, he was a presidential elector in 1820, a New York state senator in 1821, and he even served two terms as Congressman during the administration of Andrew Jackson and enjoyed the friendship of Old Hickory.

George Lee Huntington was the only son of Abel Huntington and the father of Dr. George (Sumner) Huntington. He studied medicine with his father, and after receiving his degree from New York University, he joined his father in the practice of medicine in East Hampton. He remained there for the rest of his life.

George Sumner Huntington first studied medicine as a sort of apprentice to his father and then graduated from the College of Physicians and Surgeons of Columbia University in the spring of 1871. After obtaining his medical degree, he returned to East Hampton and assisted his father in the family practice. On Long Island he was able to observe patients with hereditary chorea who had been followed by his family for several generations. Later that year he moved to Pomeroy, Ohio, and on February 15, 1872, he presented a paper entitled "On Chorea" before the Meigs and Mason Academy of Medicine at Middleport, Ohio. It was later published in *The Medical and Surgical Reporter* (26: 317–21, 1872). It reads as follows:

And now I wish to draw your attention more particularly to a form of the disease which exists, so far as I know, almost exclusively on the east end of Long Island. It is peculiar in itself and seems to obey certain fixed laws. In the first place, let me remark that chorea, as it is commonly known to the profession, and a description of which I have already given, is of exceeding rare occurrence there. I do not remember a single instance occurring in my father's practice, and I have often heard him say that it was a rare disease and seldom met with by him.

The hereditary chorea, as I shall call it, is confined to certain and fortunately a few families, and has been transmitted to them, an heirloom from generations away back in the dim past. It is spoken of by those in whose veins the seeds of the disease are known to exist, with a kind of horror, and not at all alluded to except through dire necessity, when it is mentioned as 'that disorder.' It is attended generally by all the symptoms of common chorea, only in an aggravated degree, hardly ever manifesting itself until adult or middle life, and then coming on gradually but surely, increasing by degrees, and often occupying years in its development, until the hapless sufferer is but a quivering wreck of his former self.

It is common and is indeed, I believe, more common among men than women, while I am not aware that season or complexion has any influence in the matter. There are three marked peculiarities in this disease: 1. Its hereditary nature. 2. A tendency to insanity and suicide. 3. Its manifesting itself as a grave disease only in adult life.

In this brief paper, George Huntington had clearly delineated the disease that now bears his name. William Osler, perhaps the greatest clinician of the late nineteenth and early twentieth century, wrote of this paper, "In the history of medicine there are few instances in which a disease has been more accurately, more graphically, or more briefly described."

The use of Huntington's name as the title of a disease seems most appropriate. Huntington, his father, and his grandfather had together observed the results of a Mendelian dominant gene long before any of Gregor Mendel's work had reached the English-reading world. It was this hereditary factor that was surprisingly missing from the Cooper family tree.

George Huntington made no other scientific contributions and never practiced neurology, but he always retained his interest in the disease he had described in 1872. In a speech before the New York Neurological Society in 1909, he told of his recollections of Huntington's chorea and acknowledged his debt to his father and grandfather. This paper was later published in the *Journal of Nervous and Mental Disease* (37: 255–57, 1910) with the title "Recollections of Huntington's Chorea as I Saw It at East Hampton, Long Island, During My Boyhood."

Huntington fully realized that without the facts and observations handed down to him by his grandfather and his father, whose medical lives were spent in East Hampton, he could never have formulated a picture of the salient characteristics of the disease so true and so complete as to make of it a so-called classic disease.

Old East Hampton was settled by the English in the year 1649 and was first called Maidstone, after the former home of many of them in England. They had spread eastward from Southampton, where they had landed in New England, to their settlement in East Hampton. With these earliest settlers, in all probability, came the disease. When Huntington's grandfather came to eastern Long Island from Connecticut in 1797, he found the disease already well established there, but he had little or no call to treat it, although both he and his son undoubtedly treated many choreics for other medical problems that popped up during the course of their chorea and thus were quite well acquainted with them. Years of contact with these people taught the Huntingtons their peculiarities: the age at which the disease generally manifested itself and its usually slow onset and gradual development, sometimes through a long life, sometimes for only a short period (for many of these people ended it all by suicide before its worst features had time to develop). Some worked at their trades long after the choreic features had developed, but they gradually succumbed to the inevitable, becoming more and more helpless as time advanced. Often the mind and the body both failed at an even pace.

In his 1909 speech, Huntington said he believed that the postulates taken in his original paper still held, namely: the appearance of the disease only in adult life, its chronicity and gradual advancement, its direct line from parent to offspring, and, when this line was broken, its failure to reappear in later generations. Speaking of his personal memories of this form of chorea, Huntington related the following:

> Over fifty years ago, in riding with my father on his professional rounds, I saw my first cases of "that disorder," which was the way in which the natives always referred to the dreaded disease. I recall it as vividly as though it had occurred but yesterday. It made a most enduring impression upon my boyish mind, an impression every detail of which I recall today, an impression

which was the very first impulse to my choosing chorea as my virgin contribution to medical lore. Driving with my father through a wooded road leading from East Hampton to Amagansett, we suddenly came upon two women, mother and daughter, both tall, thin, almost cadaverous, both bowing, twisting, grimacing. I stared in wonderment, almost in fear. What could it mean? My father paused to speak with them and we passed on. Then my Gamaliel-like instruction began: my medical education had its inception. From this point on my interest in the disease has never wholly ceased.

So within his own lifetime, this quiet, unassuming family physician saw his name immortalized alongside the names of those of a few medical giants as the discoverer of a new disease. Like James Parkinson and Thomas Sydenham, he had become an eponym.

I did not see Walter and his mother again for four weeks. The second visit was far shorter than the first one. I had put my patient on some medication, Stelazine, a first cousin of chlorpromazine (Thorazine—the first neuroleptic used in the treatment of schizophrenia). Stelazine, like other drugs of the class, often helps to control the movements and the emotional outburst of patients with Huntington's. It had helped him; his movements were less prominent, and he had been less agitated, easier to live with.

That was it.

As she left, Walter's mother said that she had made an appointment with a genetic counselor. Did I think that was a good idea? I did.

When it was published in 1872, Huntington's paper immediately stimulated scientific interest in the disease and in a truly scientific concept of hereditary diseases. Within a few years several physicians had tried to discover where the disease had begun, how it had come to the New World, and how it had affected the families that carried the disease with them. Brief descriptions of other patients with the same disorder were discovered. The histories of the families were traced back to 1630 and even before. Yet I could not trace Walter Cooper's disease as far back as a single generation.

In the 1630s there was considerable turmoil in England. Charles I had been king for five years. He continued his father's policy of harassing nonconformists out of the land. Under Charles I, Archbishop Laud increased the vigor with which the Church of England persecuted religious nonconformists. The nonconformists and Puritans were therefore leaving England as quickly as they could find ships to transport them. In 1630 a well-known fleet led by John Winthrop left England for American with about 700 passengers.

These immigrants included a number of residents from the small village of Bures in Suffolk, England. It seems that three men and their wives in this group brought chorea to America in their search for religious freedom. The romantic view of American history relates that the founding fathers, always pictured as Puritans, came to America to avoid religious persecution. However, pursuit of religious freedom by nonconformists was not the only reason to leave England, and Puritans were not the only English citizens being persecuted. At that time in England (and also, unfortunately, in the English colonies in the New World), it was a religious duty to seek out and destroy all of those who were believed to have a secret compact with the Prince of Hell. In Bures and vicinity, the Church of England was active in this pursuit, zealously demolishing so-called superstitious ornaments in nonconformist churches. Witch hunters assisted by bell ringers canvassed the country and received twenty shillings from the government for every suspected witch who was jailed. Only accusation, not conviction, was required before the witch hunters could receive their rewards. Witchcraft was a deadly sin, and hundreds of odd and unpopular citizens were tortured and executed as enemies of humanity. Accusations of being a practicing witch were not the only threats to the populace. The English penal code was merciless in its punishment of civil and criminal offenses. Those convicted of various crimes often accepted banishment to the colonies to avoid jail.

The fundamental beliefs about witchcraft in Connecticut

and the other New England colonies were the same as those in England. Each witch scare began with the discovery that a certain person within the community, almost invariably an adult woman, had taken on "spectral" changes in her appearance and actions. These alterations in conduct were viewed with suspicion by neighbors as evidence of familiarity with the devil, and subsequently they were reported to the authorities. The occurrence of these changes meant that the devil had already approached, seduced, and embraced the woman. The woman, in turn, had weakened under the devil's promises to defend her and finally had signed a covenant with the devil in her own blood. In this covenant, the woman gave her body and soul to the devil and thereby forsook God and the church. This was a common belief of the populace, but it was seldom admitted by the accused witch, except during torture.

The devil was believed to visit the witch at night to consort with her. While consorting, the devil would claw and scratch her, leaving conspicuous marks on her skin. She then would develop nipples in these sites of injury; these were for imps to suckle on. These imps supposedly attached themselves to her body, often hanging from her breasts and genitals.

Witch hunts may well have been one of the factors that forced families with Huntington's chorea to leave England. But merely crossing an ocean was not sufficient to escape persecution.

It appears that among the first to bring Huntington's chorea to the New World were two half brothers, Geoffrey and Nicholas Haste, and a man named William Knapp. Geoffrey Haste was a member of the court of Ferrier of Bures, and when his family objected to his chosen bride because her lineage could not be traced back to Norman times, Geoffrey and his wife-to-be fled to America, where they finally settled in Stamford, Connecticut. Once settled, Geoffrey distinguished himself in various colonial criminal records by signing, along with others, harsh verdicts on his fellow colonists. (One of these cases involved a man who was held responsible for the pregnancy of a young woman. He was sentenced to stand on the pillory to be publicly whipped and to have the letter R burned on his cheek; he was to pay the young woman's parents ten pounds; and he was to marry her as soon as he recovered. Such extreme forms of punishment were popular in those days.)

Geoffrey Haste himself was fined in court for questioning testimony against him, and on another occasion was accused in court of retaining a stolen calf. And his eldest son faced a death sentence on a charge of "bestialitie," but the magistrate decreased the sentence to two severe public whippings, a fine, and a halter to be fastened on his neck, which he was compelled to wear in public for two years. Following this punishment, the son became quite religious; he moved to another state, and many of his direct descendants became afflicted with adult chorea.

Another of Geoffrey's sons showed his susceptibility to the religious insanity of the day by acting as a juryman in the trial of Mercy Disborough for witchcraft and finding her guilty. His descendants did not demonstrate chorea.

At least one other son gave birth to a long line of choreatic individuals.

Yet another son, known in the neurological literature by the name of Jefferson, deserves particular attention. He was one of the first settlers in Greenwich, Connecticut, a community that was not in sympathy with the spirit of the Puritans. This settlement, on the border of the Dutch and Puritan settlements, served as a retreat for men considered immoral, treacherous, and vicious. In 1655 the deputies in neighboring Stamford complained to the general court at New Haven about intolerable drunkenness among the English and the Indians in Greenwich, maintaining that the inhabitants were harboring runaway servants and that marriages in the community were often irregular. In the next year, Jefferson, with a few other settlers, signed an agreement in court to yield themselves up to the lawful authorities. He later became a deputy for several years, and he retired from public life at the age of forty-four. He was ill for some time before his death at the age of sixty-one. Jefferson married the daughter of Nicholas, his father's half brother. From this marriage, at least ten generations of known choreics have sprung.

Nicholas Haste himself was not without problems. He brought his wife Ellin with him from Bures in the Winthrop fleet. The passengers on these ships had suffered from scurvy and malnutrition, which quickly thinned out the ranks of potential settlers. On landing, Nicholas was brought before the magistrates of the community for his actions during the arduous journey. He apparently had seized on the deprivations of the long voyage as an opportunity to line his own pockets. Their estimate of this quack was obviously very low, for he "was fined by the court five pounds for taking upon him to cure the scurvy by a water of no value, which he sold to a very dear rate; to be imprisoned till he pay his fine, or give security for it, or else be whipped and be liable to any man's action of whom he had received for said water." His wife Ellin, the mother of Jefferson's wife, was tried for witchcraft in 1653. She was found guilty and hanged.

Just before Ellin was to be hanged for witchcraft, she stepped down dramatically from the scaffold and whispered in the ear of Roger Ludlow, the deputy governor of Massachusetts and Connecticut. After she was cut down, she was examined by several women for devil's nipples and other anatomical evidence of her relationship with Satan. Among these women was a Mary Staplies, who had the courage to speak out and say that she had found no "witches teates" and to further declare that if Ellin was guilty, then she too was a witch. What relationship, if any, this fearless young woman bore to Ellin cannot be ascertained from records, but Roger Ludlow quickly retaliated and proclaimed that Ellin had whispered that Mary Staplies was a witch. The young woman's husband thereupon brought a lawsuit against Roger Ludlow for slander and won a verdict of fifteen pounds. In 1654 Mary Staplies was acquitted. Later, in 1692, she and her daughter, Mary Harvey, and granddaughter, Hannah Harvey, were tried and acquitted of witchcraft. In the trial of Mary Staplies, strange gymnastic performances and peculiar movements were attributed to Mary by a witness.

It is generally believed that Geoffrey and Ellin themselves had Huntington's chorea. It is less clear whether Jefferson was affected. One of Nicholas and Ellin Haste's sons gave rise to a family carrying the Huntington gene. The same happened to the family of their daughter and Jefferson Haste, the son of Geoffrey. One of Nicholas and Ellin Haste's granddaughters, Mercy Disborough, was tried twice in the witch-mania epidemic of 1692 and was finally pardoned by the justices as the craze ran its course and the authorities, perhaps out of remorse, began reversing previous decisions.

The third affected family was that of William Knapp. After landing in Boston Bay, William was taken to court to meet Sir Richard Saltonstall, a slave owner and bond holder, and it was pronounced that all future employers of William must pay Sir Richard one-half of William's wages until he had been reimbursed some nineteen pounds. It is not known if this bond was negotiated by the ship captain as payment for transportation or if it had a more pejorative basis. In any case, William and his sons were notorious principals in some of the less savory aspects of colonial life. During the first ten years after his landing, the records of Massachusetts reveal several arrests. For public profanity, he had to furnish bond for ten pounds, pending trial. For selling beer for two years without a license, he was fined five pounds. On another occasion, a payment of one hundred pounds and imprisonment were mentioned for making an offensive speech against Governor John Winthrop. In 1643 William's wife, Elizabeth Warne, was mistress of a licensed "house of entertainment" in Boston, and in the following year there was another record of a fine of five pounds against William. A daughter of William and Elizabeth married a man named Mulfoot (later changed to Mulford) and moved to East Hampton, Long Island, forming the parent stem of what proved to be the historic Long Island group of families with Huntington's chorea.

William's eldest son and his wife Priscilla were taken into custody in 1641 and charged with "distemper." Later on, this same son stole some of his mother's family silver, and the court compelled him to return it. In general, William Knapp's children were not tolerated and were publicly warned against settlement in certain parts of the colony.

William Knapp had the Huntington chorea gene, and Elizabeth Warne may have as well. They had another daughter named Elizabeth Knapp. Following her husband's early death, Elizabeth Warne left her daughter, Elizabeth Knapp, and sailed back to England and settled in Suffolk, where she was later accused of being possessed of the devil, was arrested, and even confessed to witchcraft. In the files of the British Museum, records of the complaint brought against Elizabeth Warne by one John Buttery can still be found. In these, Buttery swore that a child developed strange convulsions because of Elizabeth. The guards watched Elizabeth for three days and nights for evidence of witchcraft, at the end of which time she is said to have confessed that "she had the devil within her body" and asked that she be punished. Although there were hundreds accused of witchcraft in Suffolk in the seventeenth century, the county records give few details, and there are very few accurate historical documents of witch trials held in England before 1690. It is of interest that affected descendants of the Warne (Warren) family can still be found in the Boston area.

Like her mother in England, Elizabeth Knapp in Boston was accused of witchcraft. In 1671 the Reverend Samuel Willard, who was then minister of Groton, wrote a letter to Cotton Mather in which he described the younger Elizabeth's peculiar behavior:

> ye rest of ye family being in bed, she was . . . suddenly throne downe into ye midst of ye floore with violence, & taken with a violent fit, whereupon ye whole family was raised, & with much adoe was she kept out of ye fire from destroying her selfe after which time she was followed with fits from thence till ye sabbath day; in which she was violent with bodily motions, leapings, strainings & strange agitations, scarce to be held in bounds by the strength of 3 or 4; violent alsoe in roarings & screamings, representing a dark resemblance of hellish torm, and frequently using in these fits divers words, sometimes crying out money, money, sometimes, sin & misery with other words.

Reverend Willard, doing his duty as he saw it, questioned Elizabeth Knapp about her relationship with Satan. Under his questioning she admitted that she had been receiving visits

from Satan for three years and that he was continuing to torment her. Her consulting physician concluded that she had
"distemper" that was "diabolicall" in origin. Whether Elizabeth
actually had "diabolicall distemper," hysteria, or overt Huntington's chorea remains unclear, but her father was choreatic
and her mother came from choreatic stock.

Certainly not all of the New England witches had Huntington's chorea, but seven came from affected families and were at
risk of having it. Of these, one certainly had abnormal movements that were apparent to her accusers.

Of course, not all American families with Huntington's chorea can be traced to these three families. Another group can be
traced back to France, and its story has a familiar ring. In 1685
the Edict of Nantes was revoked, and religious tolerance in
France came to an abrupt end. Many Huguenots fled France to
avoid fanatic religious persecution. Some came to Halifax,
Nova Scotia, and brought Huntington's chorea with them.
Other families with chorea have come from Germany, Ireland,
and other European countries, including even Norway. This is
perhaps the most interesting group, because Norway is the
only country in which hereditary chorea was known and described before George Huntington's paper.

My next appointment with the Coopers did not go as well as
the previous one had—far from it. Walter said nothing. Mrs.
Cooper told me I was wrong.

About the diagnosis?, I asked.

No. About the hereditary nature of her son's problem.

It was possible that he did not have Huntington's chorea, I
countered. Without a family history, one could not be sure. But
the hereditary nature of Huntington's chorea was not a debat-
able issue.

That was where I was wrong, she said. Dead wrong. She had
seen a genetic counselor. The genetic counselor had told her
that this happened all the time, and there was nothing to
worry about. Her husband was normal. He had not had Huntington's chorea, it had just happened. A spontaneous mutation had occurred in one of her husband's sperm; the abnormal
gene had spontaneously appeared. Spontaneous generation,

she called it.

She had been told that such mutations accounted for one-third of all patients. And since it had just happened as an accident of nature, her other children had nothing to worry about. Nor did her grandchildren.

What could I say? The genetic counselor was the one who was dead wrong. If spontaneous mutation *ever* occurs, it is exceptionally rare. In fact it was not clear that the gene ever just grew in anyone. I could not prove that spontaneous generation could never happen; no one could. But if it did occur, it was rare. Very rare. I told her that.

She told me I was dead wrong, and she attacked me for pretending to be an expert on the disease.

I told her that I didn't think I was pretending. The World Federation of Neurology's Research Group on Huntington's Disease had elected me as its Secretary-Treasurer.

Then why didn't I know that there was spontaneous generation in one-third of the cases?

That was not true, I said.

But, she insisted, in one-third of the cases there is no family history. By now she was screaming at me. Her son, my patient, twitched away quietly as if this had nothing at all to do with him.

I told her the truth. The best and, as far as I knew, the only real study that had ever been carried out on spontaneous mutations of the Huntington gene suggested that it occurred only once in a million live births. The incidence of adultery, I thought to myself, was said to be higher than that. Much higher.

I refrained from saying it to her. What good would it do? Her husband had obviously been an illegitimate child. Mrs. Cooper did not have Huntington's. Her husband, the deceased father of my patient, therefore had to have had the disease. But where had the gene come from? Not from his mother, my patient's paternal grandmother; she was alive and well. Nor from his father, my patient's paternal grandfather; he too was alive and had no evidence of having Huntington's chorea. The answer was obvious: The man who was publically acknowledged to be the grandfather of my patient could not have been the true biological progenitor of the family line.

To put it bluntly, my patient's grandmother had had an affair. It was not the sort of thing one said in passing. She was now a grandmother. Her past pecadillos were long past, and only their legacy lingered on. The man who had fathered their child had not lived to age seventy-five without evidence of neurological disease, and his son had not died in an accident. Life was not that simple.

Suicide was common among people with Huntington's disease—even Huntington knew that. Walter's father must have become depressed—that too was common in Huntington's, either as a part of the disease or as a reaction to it—and gone hunting and killed himself.

What good could I do by saying it? None. So I held my peace.

Mrs. Cooper attacked. She insulted, she berated, she ranted, and she raved.

So I said it.

She called me a bastard and left. I never saw them again.

That night I reread Eugene O'Neill's *Strange Interlude*. It was in Act Three of this play that a disease remarkably analogous to Huntington's chorea made its stage debut. In this scene a woman named Evans tells her daughter-in-law Nina of the hereditary disease that runs in the Evans family. It is a dominant disease that starts in middle life and results in insanity. This disease, of course, had its roots not in classic literature but in the sufferings of families with Huntington's chorea. Whether or not Eugene O'Neill was fully aware of all the medical and genetic implications of this disease, he certainly understood its emotional effect on families that carry this gene. Such poignant scenes, in which the issue of genetic risk is presented to an outsider who has married into a family with Huntington's chorea, are still being played out today.

Had my patient's true grandfather known of the curse he carried in his genes? Had they told him? Had he told the woman with whom he shared a few illicit moments? Had it been only that? I had no answers, merely questions.

My patient's brother and sisters were at risk. They should be told the truth that the disease had not just happened. It was not the result of spontaneous generation.

Two days later I got a letter from Mrs. Cooper. She apologized. I had been right. She had been angry because I had discovered her secret after all these years. Her husband was not my patient's father.

I had *not* been right. I had made the right assumption but about the wrong person.

She too had been right; her other children were not at risk.

Incidentally, I was also right about her husband. He *had* killed himself, but not because he had Huntington's chorea. They had a fight, and she had told him that his oldest son was not his son. The father was a neighbor named Kurowski, who had died in a state hospital, chained to the bed.

Chained to the bed. In a state hospital. That graphic description leaves room for few alternative interpretations. The man had had sufficient psychiatric disease to require institutionalization, and his chorea had been so severe they had had to restrain him to keep him from hurting himself.

I had the link that had been missing. The hereditary factor was no longer absent from Walter's family tree.

From father to son, but *not* from Morton Cooper to Walter Cooper. From Kurowski to Cooper.

And Morton Cooper's wife had told him that her son was not his son. Had she told him or taunted him? Did it matter? The next day Morton Cooper went hunting and had an accident. She could live with that. She had for a dozen years.

What could she tell her other children? she asked. Was there any way out other than the truth? She could not let her children live thinking that they too could have Huntington's or could spread it to their children. What could she do?

I wrote her a letter that night. I wrote it on official stationery of the World Federation of Neurology Research Group on Huntington's Chorea. In the letter I told her I was convinced that her son's Huntington's chorea was the result of spontaneous generation of the Huntington gene and that her other children were not at risk.

Author's Note

The 1908 Huntington's number of *Neurographs* remains the best source for information on the early history of Huntington's chorea, its describers, and its sufferers. Both Russel DeJong's "George Huntington and His Relationship to the Earlier Description of Chronic Hereditary Chorea" (*Annals of Medical History* 9: 201–10, 1937) and Andre Barbeau's "The Understanding of Involuntary Movements: An Historical Approach" (*Journal of Nervous and Mental Disease* 127: 469–89, 1958) also present some aspects of this story.

The histories of the early New England families and their relationships to the witch trials have been published at least twice previously in more complete detail:

Vessie, P. R., "On the transmission of Huntington's chorea for 300 years—the Bures family group." *Journal of Nervous and Mental Disease* 76: 533–70 (1932).

Maltsberger, J. T., "Even unto the twelfth generation—Huntington's chorea." *Journal of the History of Medicine and Allied Sciences* 1: 1–17 (1961).

Of the various papers on witchcraft in New England, I have always liked Charles S. Pott's "An Account of the Witch Craze in Salem with Reference to Some Modern Witch Crazes" (*Archives of Neurology and Psychiatry* 3: 465–84, 1920).

8
Legacy

. . . The memory of all that,
No. No. They can't take that away from me.
—Ira Gershwin, "They Can't Take That Away from Me"
from the film *Shall We Dance* (1937)

Karl Allenway was the first patient I saw in consultation at Michael Reese Hospital. I recognized him immediately. We had been friends during a couple of years of high school, especially the summer the White Sox, paced by the pitching of Virgil Trucks and Billy Pierce and the all-around play of Minnie Minoso, Nellie Fox, and Chico Carrasquel, gave the Yankees a good run for their money. It was 1953, and the one thing we knew was that you escaped polio by avoiding crowds of other kids. That meant no beaches, no Riverview Amusement Park, and no more Sunday double-headers in the rightfield stands of Comiskey Park. Karl and I spent most of that summer playing baseball in the deserted schoolyards and alleys of the South Shore neighborhood of Chicago.

My mother is still certain that it worked, and she may be right—after all, neither I nor any of my friends ever contracted polio. My father, a physician, was more sanguine about it. Luck also was a factor.

Karl had not aged well. It was January 3, 1974, and we were both 37. He looked fifty. After high school we'd gone our separate ways. I'd gone to the University of Michigan and then medical school and residency. I finished my training in neurology in 1968, and now I'd been brought to Chicago's Michael Reese to be Director of Neurology. He'd gone to the University of Colorado and then to work with his father. I'd never known back in high school what his father did for a living other than make a lot of money—something to do with real estate.

Karl continued the family tradition of making lots of money and by age thirty was dying of chronic kidney failure. He had chronic glomerulonephritis, and by age thirty-one he had what his nephrologist called "end-stage kidneys." Even the most uneducated of patients understands that term. At age thirty-one he went onto chronic dialysis. At thirty-six, one year before I was asked to see him, he finally received a kidney transplant. His new kidney came from an unrelated donor, a random accident victim. The medical term for that is a rather ghoulish one, cadaver kidney. Such a kidney could not be expected to match the tissues of the recipient's body, so to prevent rejection Karl's doctor had placed him on medications that suppressed his immune system. By January 1974 he'd been immunosuppressed by prednisone (a steroid) and Immuran for about ten months.

Karl did not look healthy. His face was puffy, which I attributed to the steroids; facial swelling is a common direct effect of chronic steroid therapy. He was thinner than he had been in high school, and it was not the thinness of a conditioned athlete. Thirty-seven-year-old men didn't waste their time running or exercising in 1974. It was a thinness born out of both a chronic disease and its treatment.

We greeted each other warmly. For ten minutes we reminisced about the old White Sox, the boys of our summers of '53 and '54: Bob Elliott's great month after the Sox got him from the St. Louis Browns; ex-Yankee pitcher Tommy Byrne's ninth-inning pinch-hit grandslam homerun against the hated Yankees, a moment of sheer genius from Manager Paul Richards; Sandalio Consuegra's record-setting season, sixteen wins and only three losses.

The residents were bored to tears, so I called a halt to the nostalgia. "Tell me," I began, "why was a neurologist asked to see you?"

He took a deep breath and told me. "Weakness," he said. "I'm getting weak."

"Where?" I asked, a differential diagnosis already running through my mind. Two obvious causes sprang to my mind just from looking at him and from the basic facts I already knew because one of the residents had told me much of Karl's history as we walked from my office to the hospital. One possible cause was muscle wasting due to his steroids—a condition called *iatrogenesis*—problems resulting from medical treatment. Steroids in high doses for long times often cause muscle wasting and weakness, especially in the legs. This process, called steroid myopathy, invariably involves both legs equally and affects the thighs and hips more than the feet. Karl had been on a fairly high dose of prednisone for ten months, enough to cause weakness when taken for that long.

The other possible cause of Karl's weakness was his chronic renal (kidney) failure. This weakness was not a direct effect of renal failure on the muscles themselves. The process of renal failure instead damages the motor nerves carrying messages to the muscles. This injury to the nerves, or neuropathy, results from the inability of the diseased kidneys to get rid of various poisons or toxins. This weakness, like that caused by steroids, is invariably worse in the legs and usually involves both sides equally. There was, however, one major difference in the distribution of the weakness in the two disorders: steroid-induced weakness is proximal (hips and thighs more than feet), while neuropathy due to renal failure is distal (feet more than hips and thighs).

So distribution was the key. Steroid-induced myopathy seemed to me to be the best bet. The neuropathy of renal failure may progress during chronic dialysis but usually gets better once the patient has received a transplant.

"Where are you weak" I asked, fully expected him to say that his legs were weak or that he was weak all over.

"My left side."

"Just your left side?"

"Yes."

"Are you sure?"

He was. So much for my initial differential diagnosis. Both of my well-considered possibilities had just gone out the window, for neither steroid-induced myopathy nor neuropathy due to renal failure ever involves only one side of the body; they are bilateral or generalized disorders. The steroids and the toxins circulate through the body and reach both sides equally. Karl's problem was not in his muscles or in the nerves that carried messages from the brain and spinal cord to his muscles.

Weakness on one side of the body always implies disease of the central nervous system itself, something amiss in the brain or spinal cord. But which one? If a patient's speech or face are involved, the problem has to be in the brain itself, for the tracts that control these functions never enter the spinal cord.

"Just your arm and leg?" I asked. He thought before he answered. As he did, he pursed his lips—something he used to do back in '53. Only when he did that then, the two sides of his face moved equally, symmetrically. Now they didn't. The left side lagged behind. The question had been answered. The left side of his face was involved—only slightly, but it was there.

I knew where the problem was. Something was wrong in the right side of Karl Allenway's brain.

"I don't think so," he finally answered.

"Not your face?"

"No, not my face."

"Or your speech?"

"No."

His denials changed nothing. It just supported what I had already observed. The facial involvement, although it existed, was very mild.

So I had partially answered the first question a neurologist asks himself: I knew *where* the malfunction was. Next I needed to know the time course of the problem, not just when it had started, but its progression. Had it started suddenly? Or had it been slowly progressive? Some diseases, strokes for instance, cause sudden weakness. Others, such as tumors and infections, advance more slowly. My new differential diagnosis would depend upon knowing how his weakness started and how it had progressed.

"When did it start?" I asked.

Karl couldn't be certain.

What had he noticed first?

Some dragging of his left foot.

When?

Three or four months earlier. He wasn't absolutely sure.

When had his left arm gotten weak?

Again his answer was vague. "A few weeks ago." I tried to pin him down more exactly, but I couldn't. A rough guess was the best he could do.

I knew all I had to know. The onset of his hemiplegia (that is, weakness of one-half of his body) had not been abrupt. His condition was not due to some sudden event such as a simple stroke. His hemiplegia had crept up on him almost imperceptibly at first and had been progressing at a leisurely rate for three or four months or even longer.

Had his leg been getting weaker for the entire four months? He thought so.

Karl's weakness had to be due to a slowly progressive lesion, something that expanded slowly within the substance of the brain and as it grew caused progressive symptoms: the leg, the arm, the face. The differential diagnosis was now a list of those disease processes that grow slowly inside the brain. That well-learned list of possibilities popped automatically into my head. First on the list, a brain tumor, either a primary tumor of the brain itself or a metastasis from a cancer that was growing silently somewhere else in Karl's body. There was, as far as I knew, no evidence that he had cancer outside of his brain, but he could. He could also have a tumor starting inside his brain— some tumors in fact tend to occur more commonly in patients who are on immunosuppressive medications. Such a tumor was a good possibility.

The second possibility was an abscess. Karl was a perfect setup for an abscess. His ability to fight off any infection had been compromised by the steroids and the Immuran. Suppression of his immune system had been a prerequisite to his kidney transplant. Those same medications that prevented his body from attacking the foreign kidney now within him also prevented his body from defending itself against various bacteria or fungi that the body, when functioning even reasonably normally, easily overcomes. Iatrogenesis all over again in the guise of a slow-growing abscess.

There were other possibilities. Perhaps Karl had some other sort of inflammatory lesion, not an infection per se, nor an abscess, but a more subtle process like multiple sclerosis. Such patients usually have more than one problem, more than just a progressive hemiplegia. The *multiple* in multiple sclerosis means just that: two or more separate neurological problems—such as hemiplegia along with loss of vision in one eye, double vision, numbness somewhere in the body, or imbalance. But being on immunosuppressants did not increase his risk of developing multiple sclerosis. Just the opposite, it substantially reduced the risk, although it did not completely eliminate the possibility.

Did Karl have any other neurological problems? I pursued this possibility as vigorously as I could. I asked him specifically about each individual symptom.

Loss of vision in one eye?

No.

Blurred vision?

No.

Double vision?

No.

Any difficulty seeing at all?

No.

The list went on and on, and so did the denials. As far as Karl knew, his only neurological problem was progressive weakness of his left leg and left arm. That meant just one lesion, not two or more. A tumor or an abscess, not multiple areas of inflammation.

It was time to perform my neurological examination. The purpose of the exam was what it always is: to increase my understanding of what was going on inside the patient's brain. Defining the severity and extent of his left-sided weakness would teach me absolutely nothing. I already knew something was going on inside the right half of his brain, something that in all probability was not very good. It was the rest of the examination that counted. Was anything else not working right? Was there any evidence of something going on anywhere else in his brain? A second tumor, or an abscess, or something else? It was everything but his weakness that mattered.

I examined Karl as compulsively as any neurologist had ever examined a patient. It was closer to a dissection than a mere physical examination—from top to bottom, from memory and sense of smell to the ability to sense a touch of a cotton ball on the bottom of his soles. And I found just what I didn't want to find. I found definitive evidence of a second whatever it was I already knew he had one of.

The evidence was solid and incontrovertible. There was no other way to interpret it and no way to make it go away. Karl had a mild loss of vision to the right in both eyes. That meant that the left side of his brain was involved. Images coming from the right side hit the retina of each eye and then pass back to the brain to come together in the back of the left hemisphere.

Two lesions, not one. Number one was on the right hemisphere in the motor area and caused Karl's left-sided weakness. Number two was on the left in the visual pathway and resulted in his minor but definite right-sided visual loss.

If he had had one lesion, he might have had a benign tumor. That was no longer a possibility, because benign brain tumors never come in pairs. Whatever he had was bad.

I told Karl what I'd found and that we'd have to do some tests to pin down the exact cause. I did not go into any detailed differential diagnosis. It would have served no purpose. The workup would take only a couple of days. I could worry about all the bad things that might be happening without worrying him about diseases he'd never heard of, all but one of which he didn't have.

The workup was fairly simply: first an electroencephalogram (EEG), or brain-wave test. The EEG could not tell us what the process was precisely, but it could tell us what it wasn't. An

EEG almost invariably shows any abscesses expanding inside
the brain. The same is true of rapidly growing tumors. A deep
type of inflammation that occurs in multiple sclerosis-related
disorders does not disrupt the EEG. The brain waves are often
normal. That's not as surprising as it might seem. The EEG
records only the activity of the cells of the surface of the brain.
Multiple sclerosis (M.S.) involves the tracts deep inside the
brain.

Then we'd do one or two other tests. First a CAT scan to see
if we could actually see the image of the tumors or abscesses. If
they were really there, we should see them on the CAT scan.
Then, if the CAT scan did not reveal evidence of tumors or
abscesses, we would perform a spinal tap to see if there was
evidence of infection and, if so, to see what kind of bacteria or
fungus was causing it, so we would know what antibiotic might
work—*might* work, not *would* work. Treating infections in patients whose immune system isn't able to help is still no easy
matter. In 1974, when the available antibiotics were less potent
than they are today, the task was far more difficult.

Did he have any questions?

He did. One that had plagued him for fifteen years.

"What's that?" I asked.

"Why did they send Lollar in from third?"

I smiled. I had asked myself that same question for the same
number of years. That fateful semidash had occurred in the
second game of the '59 World Series, the only World Series the
White Sox had played in our lifetimes. The Sox had won game
one and were losing game two in the eighth inning. We were
rallying. Sherm Lollar, our outstanding catcher and the slowest
man in the league, was on third. The batter hit a short fly
ball—too short—and the third-base coach sent Lollar rambling
toward home plate. Lollar was out by a mile. That was the end
of the rally, and the beginning of the end. We lost the World
Series four games to two.

I had no answer.

"Do I have a chance?" he asked.

"More than Sherm did," I said. "A lot more."

That afternoon Karl had his EEG. It was normal. As far as I was concerned, the workup was virtually complete. The CAT scan and the spinal tap would be mere formalities. Karl did not have two abscesses, nor did he have two tumors. He was not that fortunate. It wasn't M.S. either. Being immunosuppressed decreased his risk of developing M.S. and increased his risk of contracting another form of inflammation, a disease of which he had never heard, a disease that hadn't even existed when we avoided Comiskey Park because of the threat of polio.

The disease I was sure that Karl had is called *progressive multifocal leukoencephalitis*, or PML for short. Its name defines what it is. *Multifocal* means more than one area of the brain is diseased. Karl had more than one site of disease, at least two that I had documented on his physical exam, and he could easily have had others that were in silent areas of the brain or that were too small to cause problems—yet. So his disease was multifocal.

Encephalitis means inflammation of the brain. *Leukoencephalitis* means inflammation deep inside the brain, striking not the superficial cortex but the deep white matter. (The term *leuko* means white, as in leukocytes or white blood cells.) Karl's EEG was normal because his disease was deep within his brain, not superficial. It had struck his deep white matter, not the cortex.

His left-sided weakness had started subtly and slowly gotten worse. Ergo his disease was *progressive*.

Progressive multifocal leukoencephalitis was a universally fatal disease. No patient had ever developed PML and survived, at least none that I had heard about.

Karl would not be safe at home. Unless . . .

The first case of PML was reported in 1958. Since then hundreds of patients with PML have made their way into the medical literature. Many hundreds of others have developed the disease and died without being recorded so publicly. What was once unknown now occurs at a relatively alarming rate. I see one or two patients with PML each year. It occurs only in persons who have impaired immune responses. Often the immunological deficiency results from a generalized chronic disorder such as Hodgkin's disease, and most often the patient has also received some sort of immune suppression, usually with steroids. PML is an infection of the brain that, because it occurs only in this setting, is called "opportunistic." The normal body easily resists its attack, and immune dysfunction gives it an opportunity to take hold and cause disease.

It's caused by a virus. As early as 1959 it was suggested that the disease could be due to viral infection in persons whose immunity had been impaired by disease or its treatment. The concept of an atypical form of viral infection striking patients who had some sort of immunological unresponsiveness received particular emphasis from Richardson in 1961 when he reviewed the twenty-two cases that had been recognized up to that time. The hypothesis that PML was caused by a viral infection really took hold in 1965. That year ZuRhein and Chou of the University of Wisconsin discovered that the abnormal cells in and around the lesions of PML contained numerous viral particles resembling papovavirus. ZuRhein and Chou saw these subcellular particles in the electron microscope and published the pictures. They were there for the entire scientific world to see: viruses inside the brain of a patient with PML. And not a usual human disease–causing virus, but a very strange virus—a papovavirus. Up until then the only known human disease caused by a papovavirus was hardly a disease at all: papovaviruses cause warts. The papovavirus that was discovered in the brains of patients with PML was not the one that causes warts, but a close relative.

What was the virus? Where did it come from? How did it get into patients' brains? How did it get into Karl Allenway's brain?

It took American medical scientists only a few years to answer the first three questions. It took me only a few seconds to answer the last one.

PML is caused by a virus that is now called SV-40, or Simian Virus 40. It's a virus that is normally found in simians (monkeys), not in humans. The monkey that carries SV-40 most commonly is medicine's old friend, the rhesus monkey. The spread of SV-40 from rhesus monkeys to humans had to do not with PML but with polio.

Paralytic poliomyelitis, for all practical purposes, hardly exists as an active disease in America today, for it is now preventable by poliovirus vaccines. In the United States the number of cases of paralytic polio, which averaged twenty-one thousand per year over the five years before introduction of the vaccines, fell to just seven in 1974. Similar reductions have taken place in other countries where the vaccines have been used on a large scale. No one today has to stay away from the beaches for fear of developing polio, or miss a single Sunday doubleheader. (But now, of course, there are virtually no more double-headers.)

Two types of vaccine are in use today, the inactivated virus (Salk-type) and the live-attenuated virus (Sabin-type) vaccines. Both are effective in preventing paralytic poliomyelitis. It was the Salk vaccine that first turned the tide. Generalized use of this inactivated vaccine began in 1955. In Chicago, the program started that spring. My father, a physician who worked for the Chicago Board of Health, had a lot to do with coordinating the inoculation in Chicago.

Jonas Salk developed this effective killed-virus vaccine by using the chemical toxin formalin to inactivate the three varieties of poliovirus that cause paralytic polio. But in order to do this, scientists had to grow and harvest three active disease-causing poliovirus strains. This was done by growing the viruses in the laboratory inside monkey kidney cells. The viruses were then inactivated by the formalin so that they could no longer replicate themselves. The viruses nevertheless remained intact enough to stimulate the body to produce antibodies to them. These antibodies then repel the naturally occurring disease-causing polioviruses. Because the virus does not reproduce itself inside the patient, the injected material must be sufficient to stimulate the entire immune mechanism. This requires multiple injections to produce a sufficient immune response to prevent actual disease. Immunization with the Salk inactivated poliovirus proved to be remarkably safe and effective. We were all able to go to Comiskey Park and worry about the Yankees instead of polio. They alone were more than enough of a threat for most White Sox fans.

There were two notable exceptions to the safety record of Salk vaccine. The first occurred in 1955 and got a lot of coverage in the press. Soon after the vaccine was licensed, an outbreak of sixty-five cases of paralytic poliomyelitis occurred within four weeks following inoculation of about 400,000 persons. This was traced to a single source of vaccine in which type 1 poliovirus was inadequately inactivated so that the vaccine contained residual amounts of infectious virus. This complication has subsequently been eliminated by the institution of more stringent controls during vaccine production.

The second complication was undoubtedly the contamination of the vaccine with live SV-40 virus. This simian papovavirus is a natural contaminant of the monkey kidney cells used to produce the polio vaccine. It is far more resistant to formalin inactivation than poliovirus. The formalin used to inactivate poliovirus would not inactivate SV-40. So when people received inactivated poliovirus, they also received active SV-40, at no extra charge.

So that was how SV-40 virus, a virus that lives in monkeys, got into people. In healthy monkeys it usually lives in the kidneys. We only learned that recently; we didn't know that in 1955. The same kidneys on which the Salk vaccine was grown are the natural home of SV-40. Even if we'd known that then, I'm not sure we'd have cared. SV-40 lived in monkeys, not people. There was no disease it caused in humans. Not in 1955.

And I know exactly how and when Karl Allenway got his SV-40. My father gave it to him, in the kitchen of our apartment as soon as the first shipment of Salk vaccine arrived in Chicago. My mother insisted on it. My father pulled some strings, and Karl and I and a few other selected lucky friends became the first Chicagoans to get a series of Salk vaccine shots.

It worked in general. Polio soon became a rare disease—not as rare as smallpox, but no longer a cause of annual epidemics. The manufacturers of iron lungs all went out of that business and into something else.

It worked for us individuals, too. The polio viruses entered our bodies. The viruses were too weak (attentuated) to reproduce and cause disease, but our bodies produced antibodies to all three polio strains, and we were safe.

The SV-40 virus also entered us, injected in the same syringe, through the same needle. The SV-40 viruses had been growing away, unbeknownst to anyone, in the same monkey kidneys that grew the polioviruses. The formalin, which all but killed the polioviruses, did nothing much to the SV-40 viruses. They were healthy when they entered us. So what? SV-40 causes problems in monkeys, not in healthy people. And Karl and I were healthy.

Were! Now, almost twenty years later, Karl was far from healthy. His immune system was suppressed by the steroids and Immuran he had been given for just that reason. His SV-40, which had lain dormant for all those years, no longer had to contend with a normal, healthy person. It could now cause trouble, and that's just what it had done. It had crossed into Karl's brain and done what it does best in such instances; it produced progressive multifocal leukoencephalitis.

PML is the most iatrogenic of all disease. Doubly iatrogenic. First, the virus was given to Karl inadvertently by my father when he made life safer and better for us by assuring us that polio would never strike us down. Second, twenty years later, other physicians had made it possible for Karl to live with a kidney transplant by the trick of immunosuppression. Without that second step, the SV-40 would have gone on living inside Karl's body doing no harm. It had been living that way for almost two decades.

Although the problem was iatrogenic, no one was to blame. No one knew SV-40 grew in those kidneys and wasn't killed by formalin. Even if they had, no one knew SV-40 would cause disease in people. Certainly not PML, for PML did not exist in 1958.

And Karl needed to be immunosuppressed. It was either that or endure the ongoing stress and discomfort of chronic dialysis, in which you are never quite normal and your life is not your own—hooked up to some machine three or four times a week for eight hours for the rest of your life—an endless succession of treatments punctuated by frequent complications. The kidney transplant had freed him of all that.

And now he had PML and would die. Or would he? It was just possible that he might not. There was nothing we could do about the SV-40 being in his body. But there was a lot we could do about the suppression of his immune system. For most patients with PML, there is nothing that can be done; they either have diseases that make their immune systems inactive or diseases that will kill them if the immunosuppression they are receiving is stopped. But neither of these conditions applied to Karl. Thus, it was obvious: We had to stop the immunosuppression. He could receive no more steroids or Imuran. He would, as a result, reject his cadaver kidney, but that would not kill him, for he could go back to chronic dialysis. It wasn't much of a life, but it was life. Then we could hope that his body could combat the SV-40 virus and put it back into its usual role of passive tenant, living peacefully within his body.

Would it work? I had no idea, because no one had ever tried it before. But what other choice was there? Absolutely none.

I waited one more day. The CAT scan confirmed my diagnosis, and so did the spinal tap. All in all, there was no evidence of tumors or abscesses. Karl had multiple areas of inflammation in his deep white matter, and it wasn't M.S.

I told his kidney specialist what I was proposing to do. The doctor had never seen a case of PML; he'd hardly even heard of the disease. But if I was certain, that was good enough for him.

Next I told Karl. He too was willing to follow my advice. He was not at all happy about the prospect of going back on chronic dialysis. The transplant had, in his own words, freed him. No longer a slave to those machines, he could go and come as he pleased and organize his life according to his wants and whims, not his dialysis schedule. He no longer had to worry about his shunts getting clogged up, or about a dozen other complications. He was a free man with the transplant, and he felt infinitely better than he had while on dialysis.

He talked on about this for half an hour. I let him. Then he looked at me and asked, "Do I have any other hope?"

"No."

"Then I have no choice."

I nodded my agreement.

"Will it work?"

"I hope so."

"And Don Gutteridge hoped that Sherm Lollar would be safe." We both knew what he meant by that.

"Until the ump called him out, Lollar still had a chance to be safe," I said.

That was how Karl Allenway became the first patient at Michael Reese ever to be diagnosed as having PML. It made my reputation as a diagnostician. Unfortunately, it did nothing to help Karl.

We stopped his steroids and his Imuran. He rejected his kidney within two months and went back on chronic dialysis, three times a week, eight hours each time. For one-fourth of his waking hours, one-seventh of his entire life, he was attached to a machine. The dialysis unit was down the hall from the neurology department, and I often saw him coming and going from his dialysis session.

His left side became weaker and weaker. Then he began to drag his right leg. Two months after he was back on dialysis, he needed a wheelchair. Then his vision began to deteriorate. In a period of six weeks he became blind. The last time I examined him, he was totally blind, could not move his left side at all, and could hardly move his right side. His speech was slurred. Swallowing was getting more and more difficult.

We both knew that my bold plan had been an utter failure. The SV-40 virus had not been controlled by Karl's restored immune system. His PML was destroying his brain. And he was tied down to those machines again.

"Gutteridge was righth," he lisped at me. "Lollar mighth have scored. We mighth have won."

I smiled. I knew he was right. I'd given him the only chance he had, and he'd taken that chance and lost.

In two weeks he was dead. He became the first autopsy-proven case of PML in the annals of Michael Reese Hospital.

As I watched the cutting of his brain and counted the innumer-
able areas of PML, I remembered my father giving us our first
injections of Salk vaccine in the kitchen of our apartment and
talking about the White Sox and the freedom of being able to
go to the ballpark all summer long. That freedom had come at a
cost.

By the way, polio vaccines are no longer grown on monkey
kidney cells, but on a strain of human cells called WI-38. SV-40
doesn't grow in WI-38 cells. Giving polio vaccine no longer
spreads SV-40. Somehow that is not as much of a comfort to
me as it should be. It is also of some interest that the twelve-
volume *Oxford English Dictionary* originally omitted the word
iatrogenic. That is no longer true. The editors finally broke down
and included *iatrogenesis* in the 1976 supplement.

AUTHOR'S NOTE

There is no literature on PML directed toward a nonmedical
audience. Most of what is available is fairly tough reading even
for medical scientists. The single best coherent article is probably Duard Walker's "Progressive Multifocal Leukoencepha-
lophy: An Opportunistic Viral Infection of the Central Nervous System." It was published in Volume 34 of *The Handbook of
Clinical Neurology*, edited by P. J. Viken and G. W. Bruyn (Amsterdam: Elsevier, 1985).

9
Dead Arm Dick

His name is not important. In all probability it never really was except to the faithful few South Siders who lived and died with the Chicago White Sox of old. We'll call him Dick.

I first saw him as a patient long after his major career had come to an end. He had hung on in the big leagues for just over five years—just long enough to be eligible for a pension. I recognized him the moment he walked into my office—not just his name, but his face and his record. His face looked much as it had on the Topps baseball card I had collected in seventh grade during his second year with the White Sox. The card had fallen victim to my later maturation and my mother's need to clear out my old room.

Dick had been a starting pitcher for the first three years of his career and a pretty good one for the first two seasons. Then during this third year he developed a "dead arm." His right arm (which had never been truly great) could no longer deliver fastballs for more than three or four innings. By the end of the year, he was in the bullpen as what today is called a middle reliever. In those days teams rarely had true relief specialists. The Yanks had Joe Page, but almost every other team's relief pitchers were either sore-armed has-beens or young hopefuls. In two and a half seasons, Dick had been transformed from the latter into the former. He got his two more seasons in, occasionally doing quite well for an inning or so, but never for much longer, and then he was gone.

To what? To where? I had no idea. Once he was out of the sports pages, he ceased to exist.

He looked to be in good shape. He certainly had put on fewer pounds and lost less hair in the previous twenty years than I had. He was well enough dressed in Harris tweed sports coat, contrasting slacks, and open sports shirt.

Had he become an insurance man as many other ballplayers had before and since? He seemed too relaxed for that. Maybe a car salesman? That didn't seem right. I asked him.

A teacher, he said.

Of physical education, I assumed.

No. Physics. In a junior college.

Embarrassed by my erroneous assumption, I changed the subject as quickly as I could. Why had he come to see me?

He was having trouble with his right hand. For the last two years he had been bothered by numbness and a pins-and-needles sensation in his right hand.

I pursued the history. Was his hand always numb?

No.

When did it happen?

During certain activities such as blow-drying his hair, holding a phone to his ear for minutes at a time, grasping the top of his car's steering wheel with his right hand.

And it all goes away if you lower your arm?

Yes.

Suddenly I saw Dick's entire life history being replayed before me. He was once again a strong, young right-handed fastball pitcher with a classic overhand delivery in which his right arm went almost straight up over his shoulder. No three-quarters or side-arm deliveries for him, he'd always used an overhand delivery—over the top, in baseball parlance.

He had no other real complaints. Sometimes when the numbness had been there for a few minutes, the hand felt weak. And, rarely, it became painful. And it would feel cool to the touch.

And look pale.

Yes. Cool and pale.

He was worried that he might be developing some serious problem such as multiple sclerosis or a stroke.

I nodded sagely. Those were not fears to be scoffed at, yet they were totally without any medical basis. I took him into the examining room. His neurological examination was normal, as I'd expected. After all, his symptoms cleared up completely whenever he put his arm down.

But what happened when he lifted his arm? I instructed him to hold up his right arm in the position that brought out his symptoms, and as he did so I put my finger on his radial pulse. No sooner had he raised his arm so that his forearm was parallel to the floor, than the pulse disappeared; I could no longer feel it. Thirty seconds later his hand became numb, and in another thirty seconds his hand was cold and pale. I told him to put his hand down slowly. As he did, the pulse returned, and with that the color and the warmth.

We repeated the same procedure, but this time instead of palpating his pulse, I put on my stethoscope and listened over the artery above his right collarbone. With his arm at rest I heard nothing, which is just what I should have heard. As he raised his arm I heard a noise, a murmur—what we in the profession call a *bruit*. As he lowered his arm, the noise disappeared.

He did not have M.S. He was not going to have a stroke. He had the same problem that he'd had when I was in seventh grade and he was delegated to the bullpen.

Human beings were not made to stand upright and walk, I began. And they certainly weren't made to hold hair dryers or to throw overhand fastballs. Our predecessors walked on all four limbs, their four limbs perpendicular to their trunks. When we became bipeds and assumed the upright posture without which baseball would be unthinkable, our arms became parallel to our bodies. This required a displacement of the nerves, arteries, and veins in order to get into the arms, which were now in the wrong places. This shift of location put these parts into a vulnerable position where they can easily be blocked by neighboring structures such as overly long bones or overdeveloped muscles. If the pressure is exerted on the nerve, the patient's hand becomes numb, tingly, painful, weak. If the pressure is on the artery, the hand becomes pale and cool as well as numb, tingly, painful, and weak. "It's called the thoracic outlet syndrome," I said, "because the artery nerves and veins must pass out of the thorax to get into the arm."

"That's what caused my dead arm," Dick said.

He was right. Almost forty years earlier in his life, his highly developed shoulder muscles had been pressing on the subclavian artery as it passed toward his arm. The pressure was increased by the stretch that he put into those muscles as he delivered his overhand fastball, so that precisely when the muscles of his right arm needed more blood, the artery was compressed and instead they got less blood. This happened over and over with each pitch, and soon the muscles didn't have enough oxygen and glucose, and his arm became dead.

And, of course, when he wasn't pitching his arm was normal. Since no one had ever thought of this phenomenon as a cause of "dead" arms forty years ago, three other rather unscientific diagnoses were considered then. Either he was dogging it, he didn't have the stuff to be a big leaguer, or it was just one of those inexplicable things that happened to pitchers.

The fact that his radial pulse disappeared as his symptoms appeared and reappeared as his symptoms cleared showed me that he was compressing his subclavian artery. The murmur that appeared in his neck showed that he was compressing his artery in the neck.

He was convinced it was not M.S., but what about a stroke?

No, there was no risk that he'd have a stroke.

What about J. R. Richard?

He had asked the right question. J. R. Richard had also been a major league pitcher, not forty years ago but less than ten years ago. And he was not a mere journeyman pitcher but one of the best in the game. Then, at age thirty his arm had gone out: first it tired easily and he couldn't pitch more than a few innings; then suddenly it went dead, really dead. He did not have just the tiredness that came on with effort and went away with relaxation; he had neurological symptoms that never went away—numbness and weakness. He had a blood clot in his subclavian artery, and the artery became completely blocked; no blood at all got through it, and it was dead all of the time. A few days after his arm went dead, J. R. Richard had a stroke.

What was the difference between Dick and J. R. Richard? Richard had completely occluded his subclavian artery. Then, several days later, part of the clot broke off and went up the vertebral artery into his brain and caused a stroke.

Dick understood. His symptoms had always gone away. He did not have a thrombosis of his subclavian artery, so there was no blood clot that could break up and go up into his brain. Was there anything to be done?

Other than suggesting that he use his hair dryer with his left hand, I had no ideas.

He wanted to know whether the thoracic outlet syndrome was now recognized as a common cause of dead arm.

What do you do for it?

Operate on the muscles so that they no longer compress the nerves and the subclavian artery.

Does it help?

The syndrome, yes. The pitching, perhaps. "So you might have won a few more games," I concluded.

"That would have made no difference."

"No difference? We needed every pitcher we could get."

He laughed. "It made the difference to the Sox and the fans, but I'm just as well off. I quit and went back to school, and I'm happy. If I'd stayed in the big leagues a few more years, maybe I wouldn't have gone back to school. Who knows what I would have ended up doing? And for what? A couple more wins."

To this old Sox fan, that sounded mighty close to heresy.

AUTHOR'S NOTE

The medical and baseball significance of the thoracic outlet syndrome is presented in one article:

Fields, W. S., N. A. Lemak, and Y. Ben-Menachem. "Thoracic outlet syndrome: review and reference to stroke in a major league pitcher." *American Journal of Neuroradiology.* 7: 73–78 (1986).

In it is given the complete history of an anonymous thirty-year-old major league pitcher who suffered a stroke following a subclavian occlusion. The assumption that this player was J. R. Richard is mine.

I once tried to immortalize the real name of Dead Arm Dick, but my publisher wouldn't allow it. When I wrote my first novel I was faced with what was an almost insurmountable problem for me: managing to keep the names of all of the characters straight. I'm terrible with names, and my novel was full of them—the doctors, patients, medical students, police officers, and hospital administrators all had names. The total far exceeded my limited abilities to recall names. I hit upon a brilliant solution. I would use the names of old White Sox players. Not the stars like Minnie Minoso or Nellie Fox, but those poorly recalled less-than-journeymen players who only we few die-hard nuts still remembered—the Al Kozars and Gordon Goldberrys of this world.

So it was. Sam Mele became a patient. So did Al Kozar, transformed magically into Allison Kozar. Need I tell you that Phyllis Masi had once been named Phil? And my hero, the chairman of the Department of Neurology, was of course Paul Richards, the manager whose brilliance helped to lead the White Sox out of the wilderness of the second division.

Then I blew it all. I revealed my secret to my publisher. He told me I couldn't use their names.

Why not? I was using their names in a fictional sense. No one would ever wonder whether Bob Feller had really picked Phyllis Masi off second base in game one of the '48 series.

They could sue me, he replied.

For what?

Defamation of character.

I was astounded. I wasn't sure that the characters of most of these oh-so-forgettable ballplayers *could* be defamed. What I was doing was a tribute to them.

He persisted and I relented. I changed all the names. Allison Kozar, Phyllis Masi and Herb Adams then became Marie Tooth, Donna Romberg, and Arnold "Bud" Chiari. None of them ever played for the White Sox nor any other major league team. They were all neurologists. Dead neurologists. Dead people can't sue.

You can't win 'em all.

10

The Woman Who Couldn't Watch TV

Fortunately, all the functions of my life overlap. My job description as an academic neurologist calls for three separate activities: teaching, research, and patient care. I have been lucky enough to be able to arrange my career so that it's impossible for me or anyone else to tell where one of these roles ends and another begins. I evaluate and treat patients with movements disorders: Parkinson's disease, Huntington's chorea, tardive dyskinesia, various types of dystonia. I carry out clinical research on these same patients, testing the effects of various new and old drugs on these same diseases, and I see these patients with students and residents in order to teach them about the diseases, the patients, and clinical research, but especially about treating patients with these disorders.

I had been treating Miss Claudette Pierce for almost six years when she started having a problem watching TV. She'd had Parkinson's disease for about four years when she first came to see me. That was back in the days when L-dopa was still an experimental drug. She was sixty-one then, and despite her parkinsonism, still stood erect and proud. She showed signs of parkinsonism, however. Her face, which had once been quite striking, had become stiff, cold, and emotionless. Her high cheekbones, instead of adding to her beauty, now seemed to accentuate a fierce detachment from the world. She walked slowly with small, hesitant steps and had difficulty getting out of a chair. She carried out her hand movements in slow motion, and her handwriting was small and cramped. She could hardly dress herself, buttons were a formidable task, hooking her bra all but impossible.

Her voice, too, had been altered by her disease. "I used to sing in a professional choir when I was younger," she told me. She didn't have to say any more. Her voice was soft, harsh, hoarse, and so flat that there was almost no modulation at all. It was broken and monotonous. "I sang solos," she added so softly I could hardly hear the words.

Miss Pierce was at her wits' end. She was terrified by the prospect that she would soon need to depend on others. She never had, and she didn't want to, ever.

She was a Miss in the days before the word *Ms*. had been invented. She had competed successfully in the man's world of corporate law. She had never married, but she had been asked more than once. And she told me that she'd had more than her share of male companions. She said that rather nostalgically, but there was no twinkle in her eye, and no smile crossed her lips.

Could I help her?, she wanted to know.

That, as I had learned, was not such a simple question to answer. As I probed her past history, she answered every question, no matter how personal or impertinent. There was not a hint of psychological maladjustment, much less psychosis. The more I learned, the more I admired her. She had made a conscious decision to pursue a successful career in "this man's world," and that she had done. Lovers had come, lovers had gone. Some had stayed and become companions for a while, as long as a few years. But she had always lived her life the way she wanted to. And now she couldn't. She was more than just a bit afraid. She was frightened to the marrow.

I thought I could help her. When I told her that, a small smile finally appeared on her face. That smile gave a hint of the beauty she had once possessed—the physical beauty, not the personal beauty. *That* she had never lost.

She was admitted to the hospital and became patient number nineteen—the nineteenth patient I had ever started on L-dopa—and the L-dopa did wonders for her. Within two months it was almost hard to tell that she had Parkinson's disease. Her face was full of life, and so was her voice. She couldn't sing in a choir, much less sing solos, but no one had to strain to make out what she was saying. Dressing—even hooking her bra—was a snap. Her handwriting had improved so much that her bank, which had been monitoring the slow decline of her signature, demanded a new signature for their records.

She looked twenty years younger. If I were single, I kidded her, I'd be pursuing her.

She laughed and shook her head. Being single, she told me, wouldn't help.

Why not?

I was too old for her.

Life was once again good for her. She was in control and didn't have to fear that she would lose her independence. She began to call herself Ms. Pierce. Times had changed.

My schedule was arranged so that on each Thursday afternoon I would see sixteen patients with Parkinson's disease, return patients I had been following for some time. I would see one patient every fifteen minutes, four each hour for four hours. Students and residents would see the patients first, taking a detailed history from the patients and performing whatever examination was needed, and then they would tell me what they'd learned and we would see the patients together.

On that Thursday in August 1975, Ms. Pierce was first seen by a medical student, Allison Kozar. A fourth-year student, Allison already knew that she would specialize in ophthalmology.

Ms. Pierce was doing quite well, Ms. Kozar told me—not as well as she had during the first year or two she'd been on L-dopa but still well enough to be completely independent. I could hear the patient's own voice reflected in the words that this twenty-four-year-old medical student spoke: independent. She was still independent.

Were there any new problems?

One. Ms. Pierce could no longer watch TV.

Why not?

Ms. Kozar wasn't sure. She'd checked the patient's eyes thoroughly and found nothing abnormal, so she didn't know what was causing the problem. She guessed that the L-dopa was somehow affecting Ms. Pierce's vision.

It was not a good guess. I knew what the problem had to be, and I would teach this young ophthalmologist-to-be something about the eyes. Ms. Pierce was on two medications: L-dopa and Artane. Artane had been used to treat Parkinson's for generations. It blocks the activity of another of the brain's neurotransmitters, a substance known as acetylcholine. Artane blocks this transmitter not only in the part of the brain that has to do with Parkinson's disease, but everywhere. And one of those areas where it blocks acetylcholine controls near vision, or more specifically, the bringing of the two eyes together so that the person can focus for close vision (convergence) and the adjustment of the size of the pupils for close vision (accommodation).

The answer was obvious. Because of the Artane, Ms. Pierce had a problem with either converging or accommodating for near vision, and the time when she noticed this most was while watching TV. I would teach that to Ms. Kozar, and then we could help solve Ms. Pierce's problem by lowering her Artane. All I had to do was prove that she sat right in front of her TV set and that it was a problem of near vision. The professor at work.

Ms. Kozar and I went into the examining room. Ms. Pierce greeted me like an old friend, which I was by then.

"I hear you're having trouble watching TV," I began.

"Yes," she agreed.

"When did it begin?"

"About a year ago," she admitted sheepishly.

"You should have told me before so I could help you."

She smiled vaguely and shrugged her shoulders.

"When do you watch TV?"

"Only in the evenings after dinner. After I've done the dishes."

"About an hour or so after you take your Artane."

She thought for a moment and then agreed.

So far so good. Artane often has its maximum effect one to two hours after it's been taken. "Where is your TV?"

"In my den."

"Is that a large room?"

"No, it's a small room."

Very good. "Where do you sit?"

"I like to sit in the one easy chair right across from the TV."

"Five feet away?"

"Or less."

Perfect. That was close enough to bring out a problem with convergence or accommodation. The only question was which. If the problem was convergence, she might see two images. If it was only accommodation, the picture would be blurred.

"So tell me, Claudette, exactly why you cannot sit in your favorite chair and watch TV?"

She hesitated. This was the clincher. Once she told me, I could teach Ms. Kozar exactly what was going on and show her how to examine the patient for such problems. And then I could adjust Ms. Pierce's Artane and resolve her problem. Still she hesitated.

I persisted. "Well?"

"My Uncle William."

"Your uncle!"

"Yes. He sits in my chair."

"Why don't you tell him to move?"

"I can't."

"Why not?"

"He's dead. He died in 1961."

It was, of course, a hallucination. She knew that it was and told me as much. The first time it had happened to her, it had frightened her, but it no longer did. She knew he was not really there, but his presence in that chair bothered her. She somehow knew that this recurrent vision of her dead uncle was due

to the L-dopa; she could think of no other reason. But she
didn't want to give up the L-dopa. She couldn't go back to how
she had been. In fact, she would be even worse—after all, she
had now had her disease for six more years.

Her intuition was correct. The untimely reappearance of her
uncle had to be caused by her L-dopa. I questioned her carefully. She had no other problems, no other hallucinations, no
bad dreams that she could recall, no confusion, no paranoia.
She asked me if we had to stop her L-dopa.

No.

Did I have to lower the dose?

No, but I would have to see her more often. Once a month,
not once every three months. And she had to promise me to
tell me anything and everything that happened to her, real or
imaginary, no matter how strange or crazy it seemed.

She agreed. "I must remain independent," she reminded me.
As if I needed any reminding.

The next month she told me she was having frightening
nightmares. People were chasing her in San Francisco.

Why San Francisco?

She had no idea.

Were they trying to hurt her?

No, but they frightened her. She belonged in Chicago, not
San Francisco.

On that visit I was forced to lower her L-dopa. She had been
taking two pills four times a day—with breakfast, lunch, and
dinner and at bedtime. We went down to two pills three times
a day, with the last dose at dinnertime.

She asked for some sleeping pills to help her sleep.

I hesitated. I didn't think they would help.

She did. She had tried them once or twice. She had had a few
left from a prescription that her internist had given her.

What were they?

Seconal.

A barbiturate. I gave her a prescription for twenty.

I saw her two weeks later. The decrease in L-dopa hadn't
helped. Her frightening dreams were still taking place every
night, and the same men who chased her in her dreams were

now lurking outside her house. I told her that I wanted to admit her to the hospital and stop her L-dopa completely until the dreams and hallucinations stopped. Then we could start again with a lower dose. She would probably have far fewer bad dreams and hallucinations, perhaps none at all.

She refused. We went down to one pill three times a day.

She had lost the prescription for Seconal. Would I give her another? She needed to sleep. I gave it to her: twenty Seconals.

She came back the next week. I expected her Parkinson's disease to be worse. After all, she was taking much less L-dopa. The Parkinson's disease wasn't that much worse, but she was. The men were now in her house, and they were planning to kill her.

I had no choice. I arranged to admit her to the hospital.

She asked me what I would do once she was in the hospital. Stop the L-dopa.

Could it be restarted later?

When the hallucinations and delusions cleared up.

Would she still be independent?

That I could not promise.

She went home to get her clothes.

She never came back. A friend found her dead the next morning. She had died during the night.

I assumed that she had had a heart attack. She was in her late sixties and had a family history of heart disease. Perhaps she had been frightened to death.

The next day I got a letter marked "Personal and Confidential." It was in a business envelope from the firm of Baker, Michaels, and Goldsberry. Ms. Pierce was, I recalled, a senior member of that firm.

She apologized to me. She had not done what I had asked her to do. When I had lowered her dose to two pills three times a day, the hallucination of her uncle had gone away, but she had become slower and stiffer. So she had gone back to eight pills a day.

Then the nightmares had gotten worse, with the men following her wherever she went, day and night.

She couldn't lower her dose of the medication. She had no

choice. It had not been a heart attack, it had been the Seconal. My Seconal.

Had I known? After she died—yes. When I wrote the prescriptions? No. Not consciously, at least.

Ms. Pierce, like Dr. John Lipon, developed her psychosis while receiving L-dopa for her Parkinson's disease. The two processes, however, were not identical. Dr. Lipon's L-dopa-induced psychosis had begun quickly after starting L-dopa, within the first week. Dr. Lipon, like other patients with early L-dopa–induced psychosis, had a past history of severe psychiatric disorder. In his case, he had had at least two episodes of overt schizophrenic paranoid psychosis.

Ms. Pierce's psychosis began only after four or five years of continuous treatment. Such occurrences cannot be predicted by past history, since the vast majority of patients who have this difficulty have no previous history of psychiatric disorder. Ms. Pierce had no such history.

The dream disorders were first well described in a paper I wrote with two medical students who worked with me for many months taking care of Parkinson patients. One of them is now a psychiatrist, while the other is a neurologist whose major research interest is Parkinson's disease. This study (Moskowitz, Moses, and Klawans, 1973) included many patients we saw together on the same Thursday afternoons I saw Ms. Pierce. We found that dream disturbances occurred in at least one-third of all the patients taking L-dopa for two years or longer. These dream disturbances were of three separate types: vivid dreams, night terrors, and nightmares.

In most patients these dreams were unusually vivid—all but real, well organized, and quite coherent. Most often the patient says that the dreams are neither particularly pleasant nor unpleasant, neither joyous nor frightening, and always very different from the patient's previous dream experiences. Frequently the dreams center on persons and events from the dreamer's remote past. Ms. Pierce never reported any such dreams to me, but this was before I had begun asking about the

L-dopa patients' dreams as part of my repertoire of questions. (After all, I'm not a psychiatrist.) As far as we know, most patients who have these vivid dreams recall them and are quite able to tell their physicians about them. Had she had such dreams and failed to tell me about them, as she had neglected to tell me about her uncle for at least a year?

Other patients develop what are called night terrors. These are not remembered by the patients themselves and can only be reported by other members of the family or what we would now call significant others. From the viewpoint of the significant other, the patient suddenly screams, calls out, and thrashes about while sleeping. Most patients sleep right through these episodes and the next morning are completely unaware that they ever occurred. Some patients awaken screaming yet forget why they screamed or woke up, and by the next morning are no longer aware that they screamed and woke up. Approximately one out of twenty patients receiving chronic L-dopa therapy have such experiences. Did Ms. Pierce? I have no idea. If she had a significant other in her life who could have observed them, that person never came to see me or called me.

Still other patients develop classic nightmares. These are by definition frightening, often paranoid. Like the nonfrightening vivid dreams, these are considered by patients to be distinctly different from other dreams they have had previous to undergoing L-dopa therapy. The dreamer remembers them, and they do not disrupt sleep. These Ms. Pierce developed.

Approximately one-half of the patients on L-dopa for many years have hallucinations. The hallucinatory phenomena vary greatly from patient to patient, but in any one patient they tend to become fixed or stereotyped, occurring over and over. The hallucinations are almost always nonthreatening, often occur at night, and seem to be precipitated by a bright light that contrasts with the darkness. Each night Ms. Pierce went into her darkened den and turned on the TV. The light of the bright screen then precipitated the same visual hallucination: her favorite uncle seated in her favorite chair. When she went back into the brightly lit kitchen, her uncle stayed behind in the den.

In most patients these hallucinations are only visual, but some patients have auditory hallucinations. More importantly, these hallucinations are seldom part of any overall confusional or delirious state; the patient is usually alert and in touch with reality. Ms. Pierce's uncle was not a threatening specter looming at her from a sea of monsters. He sat quietly in her chair, in her den, and watched her TV. The hallucinations most often consist of individuals and experiences that were significant in the patient's past. Uncle William had been her favorite uncle. At times, the hallucinations blend indistinguishably with the vivid dreams and are remarkably similar. At least two-thirds of the patients reporting these hallucinations have already experienced L-dopa–induced dream disturbances.

After years of these phenomena, a patient who has hallucinations and dream disturbances may start to develop a psychosis, as happened to Ms. Pierce. This psychosis is almost invariably paranoid, as hers was. The patient frequently develops a pure paranoid delusional system, although his mind is otherwise still clear and he has little or no other evidence of any generalized psychosis. Ms. Pierce, despite the men who were following her, continued to carry out the rest of the activities of her life in a completely normal way.

All of this suggests that there is a slow but steady progression of medication-induced psychiatric symptoms from normal sleep to new drug-induced dreams, then to dreams associated with hallucinatory experiences, then to a pure paranoid delusional system, and finally in some patients to a frank confusional psychosis. The actual onset of the psychotic symptoms tends to happen insidiously, and although it is occasionally triggered by an increase in L-dopa dosage, it is not usually related to an alteration in the daily intake of L-dopa. This was the case with Ms. Pierce. Neither she nor I had increased her daily dose of L-dopa; it had been kept constant. That meant that the same amount of L-dopa was entering her brain, and therefore the same amount of dopamine was acting there—an amount that had once caused no abnormal behavior and then caused hallucinations, paranoia, and mild paranoid psychosis.

Why? Unlike Dr. John Lipon, she had no abnormal receptors in her brain long before I gave her any L-dopa; she had absolutely no history of any prior psychiatric problems. If she had any abnormal receptors, then those receptors had to have become abnormal as a result of my treatment of her with L-dopa. This process has been compared to kindling a fire. It is as if the constant bombardment of the brain with the "excessive" dopamine formed from the "abnormal" amounts of L-dopa somehow alters the way in which at least some of the brain's dopamine receptors respond to dopamine. In other words, the chronic stimulation of receptor sites by dopamine or dopamine-like drugs induces a state of hypersensitivity of the dopamine receptor sites. This hypersensitivity in turn plays a role in the development of the side effects associated with long-term use of L-dopa. This result is essentially a two-step process:

1. The chronic exposure of normal dopamine receptors to excessive amounts of dopamine changes these receptors and makes them abnormal.

2. Once the receptors are sufficiently abnormal, the activation of these abnormal receptors by dopamine causes an abnormal response. The abnormal responses are the abnormal behaviors that so often complicate chronic L-dopa treatment.

The second step is not really a distinct step but a continuous increment of response from normal to increasingly abnormal: to vivid dreams, to night terrors, to paranoia, to frank psychosis. The entire process might be diagrammed in this way.

NORMAL CONDITIONS

Dopamine   *acts at*   Dopamine Receptors   *to cause*   Normal Behavior

TREATMENT

Excessive   *acts at*   Dopamine Receptors   *to cause*   Abnormal
Dopamine   Receptors

SIDE EFFECTS

| Excessive | acts at | Abnormal Dopamine | to cause | Abnormal Behavior |
| Dopamine | | Receptors | | |

Since these original observations were published well over a decade ago, a few more pieces have been added to the puzzle. Frequent disruptions of normal sleep, rather than the vivid dreams, often are the first step on the road to psychosis. A survey of our parkinsonian patients revealed prominent sleep complaints in most of them. The sleep complaints were related to the number of years the patients have been receiving L-dopa.

All in all, at least six different sleep abnormalities were found to bother the patients who were receiving chronic L-dopa:

1. Difficulty in maintaining sleep
2. Excessive daytime sleepiness
3. Vivid dreams or nightmares
4. Nocturnal vocalizations
5. Nocturnal jerks called myoclonus
6. Somnambulism (sleepwalking)

Of these, the most prominent complaint was disrupted sleep. Most of these patients fall asleep easily but frequently awaken each night and are subsequently unable to go back to sleep. The total sleep time in each day is usually adequate because patients nap periodically during the day.

These symptoms almost always precede the onset of other sleep abnormalities. Like the psychiatric problems seen during L-dopa therapy, the sleep abnormalities tend to increase in severity with continued treatment. The insomnia tends to be followed by daytime sleepiness, altered dream events, and episodic nocturnal vocalization and myoclonus, jerks of the arms and legs.

So the kindling starts slowly and builds up through many steps:

| Excessive | acts at | Slightly Abnormal | to cause | Sleep Disruption |
| Dopamine | | Dopamine Receptors | | |

Excessive Dopamine	acts at	Further Abnormal Dopamine Receptors	to cause	Vivid Dreams
Excessive Dopamine	acts at	Further Abnormal Dopamine Receptors	to cause	Night Terrors
Excessive Dopamine	acts at	Further Abnormal Dopamine Receptors	to cause	Hallucinations
Excessive Dopamine	acts at	Further Abnormal Dopamine Receptors	to cause	Psychosis

Is there nothing we can do? Is the process inevitable, its advance inexorable? Did Ms. Pierce do the right thing?

The progress in not inevitable. It can stop by itself at any step along the way. Most patients never complete the entire progression despite continuing to take L-dopa. Why some patients go on to develop psychosis and others never get beyond the stage of altered dreams is unknown. Perhaps the brains of some patients have a greater capacity to adapt or to defend themselves in some way. But even for those patients who do continue to develop new and more significant symptoms, things can be done to alter the course of the process. As soon as any significant progression down this pathway toward psychosis occurs, the dose of L-dopa must be lowered, usually by eliminating the last dose of the day. I tried to do this with Ms. Pierce. She wouldn't let me, because when she tried it, her Parkinson's got worse. If that happens and the process still progresses, or if any hint of psychosis or paranoia occurs, the L-dopa must be stopped entirely and restarted once the symptoms have cleared up.

This was what I wanted to do next for Ms. Pierce. This maneuver has sometimes been called a "drug holiday," but it is anything but a holiday. The patient is admitted to a hospital, and L-dopa is withdrawn for at least five days or until all mental changes have disappeared. After the "holiday," the medication is slowly reintroduced. Follow-up studies have shown that after such a holiday, patients can be maintained on lower doses of L-dopa and tend to show a good antiparkinson-ism effect but with a greatly reduced tendency to produce any of the symptoms of the chain of abnormalities that lead to psychosis. They sleep better during the night. There are fewer disruptions. The dreams, hallucinations, and paranoid thoughts are gone. This improvement may last for years.

It is almost as if once the kindling process has been interrupted for a while, it is possible to start all over again from the original starting point, from the original state of receptor-site sensitivity. The progression may well start again, but that usually takes several years.

Perhaps I had not explained that all to Ms. Pierce clearly enough. Or perhaps any loss of function at all was too much for her to accept.

11

New Treatments for Old Diseases

The revolution in the treatment of neurological diseases that began with L-dopa is continuing. When it all started twenty years ago, I don't think any of us knew where the trail would eventually lead, or how important it might become. Most of us were only thinking about Parkinson's disease, and mostly we were thinking about finding some new way to help our patients who were suffering from a disease for which we could do so little. The second step in this revolution was the development of synthetic drugs that acted much like L-dopa but had more prolonged and, it was hoped, more specific effects on the dopamine receptors that play a role in Parkinson's disease. Several such agents, including bromocriptine mesylate (Parlodel) and pergolide (Permax) are now in use; they have helped to further improve the lives of patients with Parkinson's disease.

Could the same strategy work in other diseases? That is what used to be called the sixty-four-thousand-dollar question. It is much more than that, and not merely because of inflation. This approach could give us a way to treat other supposedly incurable diseases of the brain. All degenerative diseases of the brain are in one sense the same. For reasons we don't understand, some but not all of the nerve cells of the brain are dying. The death of these cells results in the symptoms of each disease. In Huntington's chorea this loss of cells produces abnormal movements. In Alzheimer's disease the process results in progressive loss of memory and other mental functions. We don't know what kills the cells, so how can we prevent further cell death? We can't.

But if the cell death produces a specific biochemical change in the brain, we might be able to do something about the change. That in essence is what the success of L-dopa taught us about the treatment of neurological diseases. L-dopa does not treat the cause of the chemical deficiency; it treats the symptoms caused by that loss of one specific chemical. If this could work in Parkinson's disease, there was no reason why the same approach couldn't work in other diseases. And the suggestion that it might has been a most seductive one, stimulating two decades of intense research. This model can be viewed as follows:

PARKINSON'S DISEASE

Death of Cells of Substantia Nigra	*causes*	Loss of Dopamine	*which causes*	Parkinsonism

All that was needed to apply this model to other untreatable disorders was to locate diseases with the loss of a specific neurochemical. But did any other such diseases exist? Or was Parkinson's disease unique?

The neurochemists went to work, and the entire neurological world followed each step of their progress. And they did make progress. Parkinson's disease is not unique. Several other diseases involve peculiar, perhaps specific, losses of various neurochemicals. The best examples of these are Huntington's chorea and Alzheimer's disease.

HUNTINGTON'S CHOREA

Death of Cells of the Striatum	*causes*	Loss of GABA	*which may cause*	Chorea

GABA (gamma-aminobutyric acid), like dopamine, is a neuro-transmitter.

ALZHEIMER'S DISEASE

Death of Cells of the Basal Nucleus	*causes*	Loss of Acetylcholine	*which may cause*	Memory Loss

Acetylcholine, like dopamine, is a neurotransmitter.

We neurologists now had the handle we needed. We had two more diseases, each of which was associated with a specific loss of a single neurotransmitter. All we had to do was replace that neurotransmitter, and the diseases would be cured or at least markedly improved. Alas, it has not proved to be quite so simple. GABA and acetylcholine are both neurotransmitters and behave much like dopamine by acting at specific receptor sites, but they have been much more difficult than dopamine to replace. Neither chemical precursors (the analogy to L-dopa) nor closely related drugs that mimic the activity of these two transmitters (synthetic substitutes) have reversed either Huntington's chorea or Alzheimer's disease.

In one sense that may be more of a technical problem than an error in logic. It turns out that we were lucky in our attempts to treat Parkinson's disease. The precursors that we have for GABA and acetylcholine do not really enter the brain and replace the missing chemical, at least not in the way that L-dopa replaces dopamine. And none of the synthetic substitutes that the drug manufacturers and chemists have designed so far are very effective. But we have a correct approach, and it's an approach that we now know can work. All we need is the right drugs. The search for those is still going on.

What is even more exciting today than this search for a better synthetic neurotransmitter is another, far different approach to this entire class of neurological diseases associated with chemical abnormalities in the brain. And once again it's beginning with Parkinson's disease:

THE PROBLEM

Death of Cells of *causes* Loss of Dopamine *which causes* Parkinsonism
Substantia Nigra

THE SEARCH FOR THE SOLUTION

Stage One: ──────▶ Increased Dopamine ──────▶ Decreased
L-Dopa   Parkinsonism

Stage Two: ──────▶ Mimic Dopamine ──────▶ Decreased
Build a Better   Parkinsonism
Dopamine

But neither of these stages attacks the real problem. The cells of the substantia nigra continue to die, and as they do, it gets harder and harder to replace the increased loss of natural dopamine. The symptoms get worse. We give more medications and get more side effects. Clearly we are in need of another approach.

In many fields of medical research, the revolutions come out of the laboratory. In neurological diseases this has not always been the case. Many neurological diseases occur only in humans and can be studied only in humans. Until recently this was true of Parkinson's disease, and it is still true of Alzheimer's disease and Huntington's chorea.

Parkinson's disease is named after the first man who clearly described the clinical syndrome, James Parkinson. Parkinson was an English physician with a broad range of intellectual interests ranging from paleontology to politics, a Renaissance man living in the early years of the Industrial Revolution. In 1817 he published a short booklet entitled *An Essay on the Shaking Palsy*. In this essay Parkinson described a disease characterized by "involuntary tremulous motions with lessened muscular power in parts not in action and even when supported, with a propensity to bend the trunk forward and to pass from a walking to a running pace, senses and intellect being uninjured." While Parkinson had seen only a handful of patients with this collection of symptoms and signs, he was able to recognize that these few individuals all shared the same manifestations and that this set of manifestations went together to form a specific entity. He was the first physician seeing such patients who was able to segregate this disease as a separate entity, and he did this solely on the basis of his clinical observations of the neurological manifestations, not on the basis of the etiology or the pathology of the disease.

Parkinson's description included only manifestations of the disease that could be seen and made no reference to those that could be felt. Physicians examining patients in 1817 touched them as little as possible. In the intervening years, a few more aspects have been added to the description of the overall clinical picture of Parkinson's disease. Today four separate groups of symptoms are described as part of the symptom complex that is parkinsonism. These are tremor, rigidity, a slowness of movement called akinesia, and loss of normal, unconscious balancing mechanisms. No animal ever just develops this set of symptoms spontaneously. In the same way, no other species develops Alzheimer's or Huntington's.

But we can produce a parkinsonian state in animals. Not a slowly progressive disease in which the cells are slowly dying as they do in human Parkinson's disease, but a model nonetheless, a model in which the cells have already been destroyed. This is simple. All you have to do is kill the cells of the substantia nigra. This can be done in a variety of ways, and it can be done in any species from rats and guinea pigs on up. The model has its limits. You cannot study ways to prevent cell death in the substantia nigra. But you can study ways to treat the parkinsonism once the cells are dead.

Destruction of the stubstantia nigra makes the animal parkinsonian. Give the animal L-dopa, and the parkinsonism improves. It is the ideal way to study new synthetic drugs and to develop new approaches.

And an approach has been developed. Dopamine is a simple chemical. It is made by only select cells. These cells don't work in Parkinson's disease. Why not take other cells in the body that can make the same chemical and put them into the brain? Simple, yet totally revolutionary. The process is called *implantation*.

An implant is not the same as a transplant. A transplant consists of taking a healthy organ from a donor and transplanting it into another individual, where it replaces that same organ which is itself in some way diseased: a healthy kidney for a diseased kidney, a healthy liver for a failing liver, new hearts for old. In an implant, cells or tissues are taken from one part of the patient's own body and put somewhere else where that tissue is needed. Outside the brain, this is an old technique—moving skin around, or pieces of bone, or hair.

In the brain it's revolutionary. The brain in Parkinson's disease cannot make dopamine where it's needed because the brain cells that make this dopamine have died. So why not implant cells that can make dopamine from elsewhere in the body into the brain? The brain can still respond to dopamine if we can only get it to the right place in the right amounts. So why not implant cells that make dopamine just where it is needed?

If we use the patient's own tissue, there is no threat of rejection. The body rejects only foreign tissue, not its own tissue in the wrong place. Because of this, there would be no need for medications that suppress the immune system. With this simple operation, the machinery of the brain could be repaired.

There is only one drawback. Humans have no cells outside the brain that make dopamine as their major chemical product. But this may be only a minor drawback, for there are cells that make closely related chemicals. Dopamine is one of three related chemicals called catecholamines. The other two are noradrenaline (norepinephrine) and adrenaline (epinephrine). And there are tissues that make adrenaline—the two paired adrenal glands, one of which sits atop each kidney. A person needs only one adrenal gland to live a normal life, so one could easily be taken out surgically and put into the brain without endangering the patient's health. Once there, it could grow and prosper. Since it was the patient's own tissue, it would not cause an immune response. Once the cells grew, they would make adrenaline, for that's what adrenal cells do.

And on the way to making adrenaline, they would make

some dopamine.

Tyrosine ⟶ Dopa ⟶ Dopamine ⟶ Norepinephrine ⟶ Epinephrine
                                        (Noradrenaline)   (Adrenaline)

Perhaps the dopamine would be enough to help, or perhaps the adrenal cells would be able to fool the brain into reacting as if the adrenaline was dopamine. Why not? The brain responded to bromocriptine and pergolide as if they were dopamine.

That's the theory.

This technique has been developed entirely using animals. First is was tried in rodents, and it worked. Then in primates, where it also worked, then in humans. Without the animal work, no one ever would have tried it out in humans.

A group of Swedish neurosurgeons tried the technique in a couple of patients with Parkinson's disease. When they did their first operation, we were all very excited. It worked in animals, and it should work in human patients. But it didn't. The patients got no better. Back to the drawing board. Back to the laboratory to build yet a better dopamine.

Then there were rumors that someone else was doing implants, a neurosurgeon in Mexico City. We were all skeptical. The Swedes were experts on adrenal implants; they had been doing implants in animals for years. If it failed in their hands, how could it work for someone else? And the last scientific advance to come out of Mexico was laetrile.

But it worked. Or at least there was a claim that the technique had worked. The report, written by the Mexican neurosurgeon Ignazio Madrazo and his colleagues, was published in the *New England Journal of Medicine*. It described two patients, both of whom got remarkably better in the months following implantation.

The entire neurological world was suddenly turned on. Madrazo had done something no one else had done. He read the work of the Swedes more carefully than anyone else. The Swedes had not reproduced the technique that had proved successful in experimental animals but had used a different technique. Madrazo used the technique that worked in guinea pigs, and it worked.

One of my colleagues, neurosurgeon Richard Penn, flew to Mexico City. He visited with Madrazo and saw the patients and felt that the surgery was worth doing. We brought Madrazo to Chicago to tell us about his patients. We looked at the videotapes of his patients. Indeed, they had Parkinson's disease, and six months after the operation, they were much better. But Madrazo had operated on twelve patients, not just the two he had written about. And two others had died, one from a complication of the operation.

The technique might work, but how well and how often? What were the risks? That's what we are trying to find out. And, of course, we are not alone. Several other medical centers in the United States have also embarked on carefully designed research protocols to see whether Madrazo's results can be reproduced and to try to define who is helped, how much they are helped, and how long the improvements last.

As I write this, we have completed five implants. Three patients have been followed long enough to begin to evaluate the results, and all three of these patients are significantly improved. There is no longer any question about it. Implants can work in some patients. We have a completely new way to attack an old disease. But many questions remain unanswered. Will all patients be helped? When should the operation be done? What are the risks? How long does the benefit last? It will take years to answer these questions, and by then adrenal cell implants may already be out of date.

Adrenal cells, unlike substantia nigra cells, make more than just dopamine. So why not use cells from the substantia nigra? This is now being done in the laboratory. Substantia nigra cells are taken out of a fetus and grown in culture and then transplanted into the brain. In the animal model these work better than adrenal cells. They produce a better effect on the parkinsonism, and they seem to survive far longer. The rumor is that the Swedes will try this technique on patients in the near future.

Parkinson's disease is not the only disease that might be treated by brain implants. After all, Parkinson's is only one of many neurological diseases and one of the few neurological diseases for which there are effective treatments. This is where the excitement escalates.

No treatment has proved to be effective for Alzheimer's disease, a disorder far more common than Parkinson's disease. The possibility of attacking Alzheimer's disease with this same approach is not a pipe dream. Loss of a group of cells that manufacture acetylcholine is one of the hallmarks of Alzheimer's and may well play a role in the memory loss and confusion so characteristic of this disorder. Can we find the cells elsewhere in the body that produce acetylcholine and then implant them into the right place in the brain? Would they survive? Would they produce acetylcholine? Would the patients improve? For how long? Would there be complications?

And what about Huntington's chorea? Could we replace the lost GABA? And would it make any difference?

This is not science fiction. It's science, at its best and most exciting. It is more exciting than most fiction and far more inventive.

Will adrenal implants be an answer to Parkinson's disease? Will some other implant help in the treatment of Alzheimer's disease? Or Huntington's? Only time and careful studies will tell.

Ms. Pierce died before anyone had performed adrenal implants. Would such a surgical procedure have helped her? It's too early to know, but the hope provided by the mere existence of a new treatment might well have saved her life.

We now have a new method of attacking Parkinson's disease, a new way of treating an old disease. Perhaps it won't cure Parkinson's disease, but at least it is a major breakthrough. I'm confident that somewhere out there there is a neurologic disease that cell implants will cure, probably more than one—if not Parkinson's then Alzheimer's, Huntington's, or some other disorder that up until now has been untreatable. Which disease or diseases remains unknown, but the game is afoot.

Author's Note

The only published article on successful adrenal implants in Parkinson's disease is the one published by Madrazo and his colleagues in the *New England Journal of Medicine* (316: 831–35, 1987). The less scientifically inclined reader may be interested in my second novel, *Informed Consent* (Signet, 1986). The book centers upon several patients who received experimental brain implants for the treatment of neurological diseases, including a substantia nigra implant used in a patient with severe Parkinson's disease.

Few of the questions about the long-term effects of implants on Parkinson's disease can be answered by any one investigator studying a few highly selected patients. Fortunately, most of the neurologists and neurosurgeons working on implants are well aware of this and have agreed to participate in a cooperative registry of all patients undergoing this procedure. This registry is being sponsored by the United Parkinson Foundation of Chicago, Illinois. All of us who are studying this problem thank them for their support. Our own work on implants is also a cooperative venture involving one neurosurgeon (Richard Penn), four neurologists (Christopher Goetz, Caroline Tanner, Kathleen Shannon, and me), two neuropsychologists (Robert Wilson and David Gilley), and a neuropharmacologist (Paul Carvey).

Life was much simpler in 1968 when I was the first neurologist in Chicago to give L-dopa. I was a one-man team in those days. All of us tend to look back at simpler times with a great deal of nostalgia. The fact is that today one person working alone cannot adequately carry out major clinical research studies. I am fortunate to be associated with so many excellent young investigators. Still, the good old days were fun.

12

Giants Among Men

I never saw Bill Simonovich as a patient. I never took his medical history or examined him. There was no need to—his diagnosis was obvious just from looking at him. As a freshman in medical school, I was able to diagnose his disease correctly, and the only evidence I had was what I remembered from having seen him several years earlier on television. He looked precisely like the photographs in the textbooks; they could easily have been of him.

Bill Simonovich was a center on the basketball team of the University of Minnesota in the early fifties. It was a pretty good team—not an NCAA championship team or even Big Ten champs, but a good team. Simonovich, the big man in the middle who dominated the game, was 6'11" and weighed well over 260 pounds. He couldn't jump very well, but he filled up the small lane in the center of the court, and he could put the ball in the basket, averaging some twenty points per game as a freshman.

Two separate and seemingly unrelated events combined to bring about a quick and premature end to his successful career as a basketball star. First, college basketball rulemakers made the free-throw lane wider. When Simonovich was a freshman, the free-throw lane was several feet narrower than the free-throw circle. The entire area carried the name "the keyhole," since that was what it resembled. The powers that be made the lane the same width as the circle, and it still has those same dimensions today.

That change in the keyhole, which had been there for generations, was called the Russell Rule, for it was designed to keep Bill Russell, the greatest player of his and perhaps any time, farther from the basket. The three-second rule, which strictly limited to three seconds the time an offensive player could stay within the confines of the free-throw lane, stayed on the books. So did the rule that on free throws no one could stand within the lane. From then on Bill Russell had to stand two feet farther from the basket. The change had no effect on Russell; mere mortals couldn't overcome Russell by just changing the rules. The San Francisco Dons led by Russell again went undefeated and won yet another NCAA championship.

I always thought of the new rule as the Simonovich Switch, not the Russell Rule, for it affected Big Bill Simonovich far more than it did Russell. The change destroyed Simonovich and his Minnesota team. The lane was too wide for Simonovich. By the time his sophomore season began, he could hardly cross the widened free-throw lane in the required three seconds. He could not dominate the boards from that distance, and he could hardly ever score from that far out. The next year he played little more than one minute a game.

But more than the rulemakers had caught up with Simonovich; so had his disease. The same one that had made him All Big Ten as a freshman now made him too weak to lift his heavy frame off the floor and too slow to adapt to the newly widened lanes.

We are all taught to think of diseases as bad things that can only do harm. In the long run that is probably true; no disease that I know of increases life expectancy. But for a while at least, some diseases can appear to be beneficial. One such disease can make the patient bigger, taller, stronger, capable of dominating a basketball court or a boxing ring like the once famous Primo Carnera did, or even able to seize control of the entire civilized world.

This disease, the one that both started and ended the career of Big Bill Simonovich, is *acromegaly*. Acromegaly was first described as a disease state in 1886 by Pierre Marie (1853–1940), a French neurologist. At that time Paris was the most renowned center for neurology in the world. That position had been brought about by the remarkable achievements of Jean-Martin Charcot, who held the world's first professorship in neurology. One of Charcot's most successful disciples, Marie was able to delineate the disease and its manifestations by using the tools of observation he had learned from Charcot. He coined the term *acromegaly* to describe this "new" disease.

The word *acromegaly* itself comes form two Greek words: *akron*, which means extremity or extreme, and *megale*, which means great. Marie applied his new word to patients who manifested great growth of the distal or extreme ends of their body parts. To this day, it is used to define this now well-known clinical disorder characterized by enlargement of the extremities, especially the hands and the feet, as well as the nose and jaw. Acromegaly not only makes a person uncommonly large, but it also causes a specific pattern of growth at the ends of bones that results in the peculiar body features that characterize all patients with acromegaly. Thus clinicians can diagnose the disease by merely seeing a patient. One look at Bill Simonovich trying to play center for Minnesota's Golden Bears, and the diagnosis was obvious. One look at Primo Carnera in the ring was all the trained clinician ever needed.

Marie not only characterized the clinical manifestations of acromegaly, but also showed that the disease was caused by a tumor of the pituitary gland. The pituitary gland is a very small gland that rests in the skull just below the brain. The pituitary is often called the master gland, and in a way it is. In conjunction with the hypothalamus, the part of the brain just above it, it helps to control the function of many of the other endocrine glands spread throughout the body. It also produces a hormone that controls growth. This hormone is called, simply enough, the growth hormone.

It is now known that the extraordinary overgrowth of bone and the connective tissue of the skin and subcutaneous tissues that characterizes acromegaly is the result of excessive production of growth hormone by a pituitary tumor. If Bill Simonovich had acromegaly, then he had to have had a tumor in his pituitary gland. And Primo Carnera must have as well.

If the tumor becomes active and begins secreting excessive amount of growth hormone before the age at which the growth centers of the long bones of the arms and legs become joined, the bones grow enormously in all their dimensions, and they result in gigantism, not just acromegaly. The patient becomes tall, thick, and heavy, a veritable giant. This syndrome, in which not just the ends of the bones grow but the entire body, is called *pituitary gigantism*.

If the disorder begins after these growth centers of the bones have united, the overgrowth is confined to the ends of the bones, producing acromegaly. If the tumor begins closure of the growth centers and continues its active production afterward, the patient manifests both gigantism and acromegaly. This combination of pituitary gigantism and acromegaly was first described by another of Charcot's students, Henri Meige.

So acromegaly made Bill Simonovich 6'11" and muscular enough to hold his own against the other big men in the center of the court. Acromegaly also made Primo Carnera big and tough-looking.

But patients with acromegaly are never fast. Speed was not one of Simonovich's or Carnera's major attributes. When Carnera finally fought a legitimate fight, after a number of apparently fixed fights, he was outclassed.

Although Marie did not define this disease until 1886, like most other diseases it existed long before physicians were smart enough to recognize it. Marie did not invent acromegaly: he discovered and described it. He separated it from the myriad other diseases that afflict people and thus made it possible for others to diagnose it, study it, and eventually treat it.

Simonovich and Carnera were not the only ones whose lives

had been changed by acromegaly. One look at an ancient coin of a Roman emperor named Maximinus, and it's obvious that, 1,650 years before Marie's discovery, Maximinus had the same disease. Like Simonovich and Carnera, the disease at first benefited his career. And just as it ended the short athletic careers of the other two, it finally undoubtedly contributed to his downfall.

For hundreds of years, collectors of Roman coins have been aware of the distinctive, if not peculiar, profile of Maximinus I, emperor of Rome from A.D. 235 to 238 (Figure 1). The coin portraiture of this emperor clearly illustrates his heavy features, especially a prominent supraorbital ridge above his eyes and a markedly protruding lower jaw, called *prognathism*. This could be a profile of Bill Simonovich, Primo Carnera, or any other patient with acromegaly. These features, taken together, lead inescapably to a clinical diagnosis of acromegaly.

Maximinus attracted the notice of Emperor Lucius Septimius Severus (Figure 2) (A.D. 193–211) because of his extraordinary size and strength, and he was given a commission in the Roman army. During the reign of Severus, Maximinus attained the rank of centurion and was held in high esteem by Severus, who was considered by all sources to be an excellent judge of other men. At his death, Severus left the empire to his two sons, Caracalla (Figure 3) and Geta (Figure 4). After only one year, Caracalla arranged for the assassination of Geta and became the sole emperor of the Roman world. Caracalla's reign was marked by increasing cruelty and extravagance. In A.D. 217 he was murdered on the orders of the praetorian prefect Macrinus (Figure 5), who was subsequently proclaimed emperor. Following the murder of Caracalla, Maximinus apparently left the army. In his mammoth work, *The Decline and Fall of the Roman Empire*, Edward Gibbon, basing his conclusions on *Scriptores Historia Augustae*, explained Maximinus's resignation of his commission in these words: "Gratitude forbade Maximinus to serve under the assassin of Caracalla."

Macrinus reigned for only one year and was followed in rapid succession by a thirteen-year-old named Elagabalus (Figure 6) and then by Severus Alexander (Figure 7). The reign of

Lucius Septimius Severus	A.D. 193–211
Caracalla, son of Septimius Severus	A.D. 211–217
Geta, son of Septimius Severus, murdered by Caracalla	A.D. 211–212
Macrinus	A.D. 217–218
Elagabalus	A.D. 218–222
Severus Alexander	A.D. 222–235
Maximinus I	A.D. 235–238

Figure One.

Sesterius of Maximinus. MAXIMINUS PIVS AVG GERM. AVG: abbreviation for Augustus, which was the most distinctive title of the emperor. GERM: abbreviation for Germanicus, an honorary title given in reference to victories over German tribes. Often this title was also hereditary.

Figure Two.

Sestertius of Septimius Severus. SEV PERT AVG IMP V. SEV: abbreviation for Severus. PERT: abbreviation for Pertinax, predecessor of Septimius Severus as emperor. IMP: abbreviation for Imperator, a title of acclamation for victories of the emperor or his subordinates.

Figure Three.

Sestertius of Caracalla. M AVREL ANTONINUS PIUS AVG GERM.

Figure Four.

Sestertius of Geta. IMP CAES P SEPT GETA PIUS AVG. CAES: abbreviation for Caesar, until adopted by all emperors and given to heirs to the throne.

Figure Five.

As of Macrinus. IMP CAES M OPEL SEV MACRINUS AVG.

Figure Six.

Sestertius of Elagabalus. IMP CAES M AVG ANTONINUS PIUS AVG.

Figure Seven.

Sestertius of Severus Alexander. IMP SEV ALEXANDER AVG.

Severus Alexander lasted some thirteen years. This effeminate Syrian youth, who was under the thumb of his strong-willed mother Julia Mamaea, became increasingly unpopular with the army. In A.D. 235 the well-loved Maximinus was proclaimed emperor by the army, and Severus Alexander was killed.

Within three years of his accession, the once-popular hero was considered to be a tyrant comparable to Caligula or Nero. According to all ancient sources, his behavior was more monstrous than Caracalla's. His cruelty was unbounded and was said to be exceeded only by his suspicious nature. Gibbon accused this once-honorable man of murdering many of his benefactors, leaving an indelible history of his baseness and ingratitude. In the end, Maximinus was killed by the army.

So much for the life and times of Maximinus, for three years the emperor of the Roman Empire. His entire life was undoubtedly dominated more by his disease than by the vagaries of the rest of the Roman world. At least three peculiar features stand out. The first was his prodigious size and strength; he could have been a center for the Thracian national basketball team, had such a sport or such a team existed. The second feature is his early record of honor, gratitude, and personal loyalty, and his ability to stimulate the love and loyalty of the army. The third is his subsequent record of unbridled ambition, cruelty, and paranoia that produced hatred and disloyalty among the same troops who only a few years earlier had proclaimed him emperor.

Historians have tended to give psychological explanations of this change in personality, but physical cause is far more probable. In fact, it is far more likely that the same disease that made his unprecedented success (he was the first foreign-born Roman citizen to be proclaimed emperor) also led to his downfall. It was all the result of a pituitary tumor.

Maximinus, like Bill Simonovich, appears to have manifested both aspects of excessive production of growth hormone by a pituitary tumor—gigantism beginning in early life and adult acromegaly. Historical sources all agree that Maximinus was a giant, with reports of his height varying from 7'2" to 8'6". As late as the 1960s, when the average height was certainly greater than it was in the second and third centuries, it was generally taught that among Caucasians a body height in excess of seven feet almost always indicates a pituitary tumor that is secreting growth hormone. This must also have been true 1,700 years ago.

The reports of Maximinus's height are accompanied by tales of his prodigious strength. Although as it progresses, acromegaly is usually associated with weakness, there have been numerous reports of patients who were unusually strong early in the course of the disease and later gradually became weaker. In fact, Pierre Marie reported on one such patient in his original paper.

Thus it is important to note that, although Maximinus was reported to have exceptional strength, the descriptions of his strength derive from the period before his resignation from the army in A.D. 217 and mostly have to do with his initial meeting with Septimius Severus around the year 206. Borrowing directly from ancient sources, Gibbon retold these stories as follows:

> The Emperor Severus, returning from an eastern expedition, halted in Thrace, to celebrate, with military games, the birthday of his younger son, Geta. The country flocked in crowds to behold their sovereign, and a young barbarian of gigantic stature [Maximinus] earnestly solicited, in his rude dialect, that he might be allowed to contend for the prize of wrestling. As the pride of discipline would have been disgraced in the overthrow of a Roman soldier by a Thracian peasant, he was matched with the stoutest followers of the camp, sixteen of whom he successively laid on the ground. His victory was rewarded by some trifling gifts, and a permission to enlist in the troops. The next day, the happy barbarian was distinguished above a crowd of recruits, dancing and exulting after the fashion of his country.

Here is a man who could have been not only All Big Ten but All World on any basketball team, Russell Rule or no Russell Rule. Or, like Primo Carnera, he might have competed for the heavyweight crown. However, he had far different goals.

Available ancient sources report no extraordinary physical

feats when Maximinus resumed his career under Severus Alexander in A.D. 222. All reports after this date concern Maximinus's administrative ability.

The prodigious strength that can characterize gigantism does not last forever. The sufferer becomes slower and weaker. The bones become thicker and heavier and so, harder to lift. The muscles increase in bulk but not strength. Jumping and running become more difficult as the patient's bulk increases. Then true weakness sets in. This weakness is due to progressive nerve disease, as the nerves thickened by acromegaly begin to have difficulty transmitting their messages to the muscles. The patient can no longer jump; stuffing a basketball becomes impossible; the Russell Rule becomes an insurmountable barrier. Back to the bench.

The manifestations of acromegaly are quite characteristic. There is progressive enlargement of the bones and soft parts that is most marked in the hands and feet, resulting, for instance, in broad, thick "gingerbread hands." In this regard it is particularly interesting to note that Maximinus's thumb was reported to be so thick that he used his wife's bracelet for a ring. Such extreme thickness of the fingers and thumb is characteristic of acromegaly. Acromegaly also has characteristic effects on the skull and face. The skull becomes enlarged and thickened, and all its bony ridges are exaggerated; the margins of the orbits, including the supraorbital ridge, the cheekbones, the external occipital protuberance, and, most striking of all, the lower jaw, become enlarged. The mandible begins to jut out significantly, resulting in prognathism. These features are clear on the portraits of Maximinus on his coins.

According to the *Scriptores Historia Augustae*, in a single day Maximinus could drink an amphora (about seven gallons) of wine and eat thirty or forty pounds of meat. Such thirst (polydipsia) and hunger (polyphagia), although undoubtedly exaggerated by this anonymous and at times wretched biographer, are far beyond the appetites attributed to other ancient heroes of noted strength and size. Polydipsia and polyphagia are, of course, two of the three cardinal symptoms of diabetes mellitus. The third is plyuria (excessive urination), which must occur in anyone who consumes anywhere near seven gallons of fluid per day. Approximately 20 to 40 percent of acromegalics develop diabetes mellitus as a complication of their acromegaly, for one of two reasons: blockade of the action of insulin in the various tissues of the body, or exhaustion of the cells that manufacture insulin in the pancreas. The increased consumption of food and liquid attributed to Maximinus could well have resulted from acromegaly-induced diabetes mellitus. Again the coin portraiture is of some help, because Maximinus's prodigious intake of food clearly was not associated with any evidence of obesity. This is most consistent with acromegaly-induced diabetes, in which increased appetite and food consumption result in no weight gain.

Most of the clinical problems caused by pituitary tumors result directly from the growth hormone produced by the tumor. Such tumors can also produce symptoms by a second mechanism. The progressive slow growth of a pituitary tumor can cause pressure on neighboring structures, including the base of the brain, especially the hypothalamus, which lies directly over the pituitary. Extension of the tumor to involve the hypothalamus could help explain other aspects of Maximinus's career.

The monstrous change in Maximinus once he became emperor is difficult to comprehend on purely psychiatric grounds, but such changes in behavior have been described in patients with tumors involving the hypothalamus. Such patients can manifest increased emotional excitability, even building up to severe rage attacks, and aggressive behavior precipitated by paranoid ideation has been described as a characteristic sign of a tumor involving the hypothalamus. These patients can react to insignificant events with excessive states of excitement, and they are capable of indiscriminate attacks against anyone who happens to be present. Some of these patients have described this condition as a feeling of rage building up in spite of their efforts to control it, until it conquers their thoughts and leaves them no choice but to let it freely run its course. Other patients with this condition appear to wait in a state of tension for the first opportunity to release their accumulated aggressiveness.

It is tempting to speculate that Maximinus's pituitary tumor began to expand out of the sella turcica (the bony vault in the skull that houses the pituitary gland) and slowly impinge on the hypothalamus. This would account for the vicious paranoid behavior that marked his cruel reign and led to his final destruction.

Absolute diagnosis, of course, would require an examination of the skeletal remains of Maximinus, but alas this will never be possible. There is no chance that his body will ever be found, for after Maximinus and his son were murdered, "Their bodies were thrown out for anyone to desecrate and trample on before being left to be torn to pieces by dogs and birds." The heads of Maximinus and his son were then sent to Rome and further desecrated before being thrown into the Tiber. If his skull had not been lost, the diagnosis would not need to be based on observations of his physical characteristics alone; it could be supported by a careful examination of his sella turcica.

This has been done before. A similar diagnosis was made by the godfather of all we know about pituitary tumors, Harvey Cushing, who examined the skull of John Hunter's giant only 150 years after the giant's death.

Hunter (1728–1793) is generally considered to have been one of the greatest surgeons in the history of the United Kingdom, and he has often been referred to as the founder of scientific surgery. His numerous papers and publications did much to give the field of surgery a scientific outlook. As one of his contemporary surgeons wrote of him, "He alone made us gentlemen." Much of his time and energy, however, were spent in amassing his once-famous collection, which, while not peculiar for its time, strikes us today as quite strange. It was as much a menagerie as a scientific display of anatomical dissections. Additions to his collection often were sought after specifically because of their strangeness or grotesqueness. During his life, Hunter acquired and kept a host of live specimens, including leopards, snakes, buffalos, bats, jackals, zebras, and an ostrich. Today, when many English estates have been turned into wildlife preserves as tourist attractions, one might not be surprised to find such a variety of animals in a country mansion. But Hunter's home was the first such preserve, and his motive was not monetary gain, but an insatiable eclectic curiosity. His dead specimens included a famous racehorse and a greyhound that had belonged to a man of distinguished rank.

Hunter's zeal as a collector knew no bounds. From the time he first heard about the Irish giant named O'Brien, Hunter coveted his remains. When the giant fell sick, Hunter knew his opportunity was near, and he spared neither time nor money. He was absolutely determined to have O'Brien's skeleton in his collection. As the giant was nearing death, Hunter had one of his assistants named Howisen keep a twenty-four-hour watch over the dying man. The Irishman, however, knew something was afoot, and he was equally determined that his body would not be dissected and displayed. He arranged for his friends and an undertaker to keep a constant watch over his body from the time of death until a lead coffin could be built and his body sealed in it and buried at sea. Hunter offered the undertaker a bribe of 500 pounds, and soon after his death, O'Brien's body became part of the Hunter collection. In classic Hunter style, the giant's skeleton was displayed beside the skeleton of a Sicilian dwarf (1'8").

In 1909 Harvey Cushing, the first and greatest of all neurosurgeons, visited the Hunter collection, which had been purchased by the government upon Hunter's death and had become the basis of the collection of the Royal College of Surgeons. Cushing examined the skull of Hunter's giant and found that the sella turcica was eroded and that this erosion had been caused by a pituitary tumor.

Thus, O'Brien's acromegaly-gigantism was due to a pituitary tumor, and the Irish giant, who died more than one hundred years before Marie's original paper, became the first proven case of pituitary acromegaly. The local inhabitants of the community where O'Brien had been born had a different interpretation. They attributed the giant's extraordinary size to a supernatural influence on the site of his conception, although it is unclear how the specific site was known to them.

AUTHOR'S NOTE

The historical data presented here were for the most part derived from three sources:

Scriptores Historia Augustae, trans. D. Magie. Cambridge: Harvard University Press, 1968. This is a collection of biographies of Roman emperors, claimants to the throne, presumptive heirs, and colleagues from the time of Hadrian (A.D. 117) to Numerianus (A.D. 284). It was apparently compiled by six different anonymous authors between the years 285 and 335. The credibility and value of the individual biographies have been much debated.

Gibbon, E. The Decline and Fall of the Roman Empire. Monder Library, 1932.

Herodian. History, trans. C. R. Wittaker. Cambridge: Harvard University Press, 1969. The History of Herodian covers a period of the Roman Empire from the death of Emperor Marcus Aurelius (A.D. 180) to the accession of Gordian III (A.D. 238) just following the death of Maximinus. Most other sources for this period have been lost, so that Herodian's History is the only contemporary history of this era that has survived intact.

All coins illustrated here are from the collection of the author and were photographed by Harlan J. Berk, Ltd. The rendering of the coin inscriptions was done according to Z. H. Klawans, Reading and Dating Roman Imperial Coins (Racine, Wisc.: Western Publishing, 1977).

13

The Rule of Three

Even though physicians receive many years of scientific training, including a thorough indoctrination in the scientific method and the scientific process of logic as well as a reasonable grounding in statistics, American medicine has retained its own bits of folklore. These have no scientific basis, yet are believed throughout the United States and continue to be passed on wherever interns are taught. This veritable mythology has become part of the rites of passage from medical student to fully trained physician, transmitted from generation to generation like the ability to put in a central venous catheter or the skill to do a spinal tap in a patient whose back is bent by arthritis and whose spine is hidden by fat. No available textbook lists these so-called facts; they are learned as part of the apprenticeship of young physicians.

One of the most firmly entrenched of these beliefs is that rare diseases, unexpected complications, and Iatrogenic disasters come in threes. I suppose now this general rule has been expanded to include malpractice suits.

I have always been skeptical of the first of these applications of the Rule of Three. Neurology as a specialty is full of rare and uncommon diseases. Over the past twenty years I must have seen at least one person each week who had what is usually classified to be a rare disease. When a second patient arrives in my office that same week with the same disease, I consider that to be no more than a coincidence. And when the third one shows up, I usually assume the disease is not as rare as I had been led to believe.

The first week of May in 1972, I saw a patient named Carol Lockman, a psychiatric social worker and the wife of a psychiatrist. When I saw her, I of course had no idea that there were to be two more patients like her.

Mrs. Lockman was thirty-two then; her husband, Walt, was a couple of years older. I had known him professionally for about three years but had never met her before. They'd been married for about six months. She was pale, drawn, and in obvious distress. I let her husband do most of the talking. I rarely do that—firsthand information from the patient is almost always of more value—but she didn't look quite up to it.

His wife had felt perfectly well that morning, Dr. Lockman began. The night before they had made love, and it had been fine. It had caused no problems.

I had no idea why he had to tell me that. Their love life was of no particular neurological significance.

They had had breakfast early, as usual, and gotten to their respective offices at eight o'clock in order to see patients who had appointments early in the day. He had then picked her up at ten-thirty so that they could go to the funeral of an aunt she hadn't seen in many years, a woman they hadn't even invited to their wedding. At the funeral Carol had seemed fine.

I looked at Carol to see whether she agreed. She nodded very weakly. Her color and appearance had not improved any; her complexion was almost as bleached out as her long, all but whitish hair.

The funeral service itself was short. Neither of them had any desire to drive all the way out to the cemetery. Besides, he had to make rounds in the hospital at twelve-thirty, and they couldn't get out to the cemetery and back in just over an hour.

Again I did not understand his detailed explanation. What difference did the exact time make?

They had gone directly back to his office. It was just after twelve when they got there. His secretary, Mrs. Koslo, was at lunch. She wouldn't be back until one. It had, he emphasized, all been Carol's idea. He'd rejected it at first but then gave in. Why not, if she really wanted to?

"What was her idea?" I asked.

"Making love on the couch in my office," he admitted slowly, then added with a rush, "where my patients lie down for analysis."

"Oh," I responded. "A quick matinee in the office."

"Yes," he concurred. "Very quick. She never even took off her clothes. She just rolled down her panty hose. I . . . I . . . didn't even take off my pants." He paused. "It was exciting for both of us. We'd never made love that way. With our clothes on. Or in my office. On that couch. Or in such a hurry. It was . . . it was quite an experience."

"For both of you?" I asked. Their harmless adventure had captured my interest.

"Yes," she said softly. "The best."

"I guess it's too bad I don't have a couch in my office," I joked. "An examining table is not the same." Neither of them found my attempt at humor the least bit funny.

"That's when it happened," he informed me.

"What?"

"The headache!"

"What headache?" I was surprised.

"Her headache," he explained.

"A headache," I repeated.

"Yes."

"When?"

"Right after I . . . had my orgasm," she said.

"It was the worst headache she ever had," he said.

It was time to ask her some questions directly. Secondhand data would no longer suffice.

The pain, she told me, had begun within one minute of her orgasm. The orgasm had been very intense, as intense and pleasurable as any she could recall. The whole episode had been a real turn-on, until the headache had started.

I asked her to describe the pain as well as she could. Severity, character, location.

Intense, she said, the worst headache of her life—throbbing, pounding, like a heartbeat. In the back of her head.

Both sides?

No. Just on the right.

Were there any other symptoms?

Nausea—the feeling that she wanted to throw up. She also felt weak all over and tired. She wanted to go to sleep.

Had she ever had a headache anything like that before?

She hesitated ever so briefly and then said, "No. Never."

"Was the headache the first thing that happened?"

"No," she said. "I saw stars. Right when I had my climax. I saw stars."

"Did that ever happen before?"

"No."

"Were they everywhere?"

"No, just to the left. Bright stars, all different colors, flashing on and off. They lasted for a minute or so, and then my head started to pound."

"Then what happened?" I asked.

The headache was immediately followed by an argument. She told her husband about the pain and he, good analyst that he was, figured it was psychosomatic, if not overtly neurotic— a result of the time, the place, the sequence, the guilt. She was sure it wasn't. She made him call their internist, Larry Jansen.

Dr. Jansen agreed with her. His opinion had not helped the situation. He'd had one patient, a man named Jim Hearn, who'd gotten the worst headache of his life at the time of an orgasm. That headache had been the result of the rupture of a blood vessel in his head, and Mr. Hearn had died from it. Not exactly a reassuring story. Neurosis was better than that, so they came to see me.

Mr. Lockman wanted me to confirm his theory and tell him that his wife's headache was nothing serious, just a little guilt manifesting itself. A quickie on the way home from her aunt's funeral is not the thing a nice girl should do.

His wife knew he was wrong, but she also wanted Dr. Jansen to be wrong.

The headache she described was a classic migraine. Had she ever had migraine headaches before?

No.

Had anyone in her family?

No.

Was she sure she'd never had a headache like that before? She was sure. If she had, she'd remember them.

Why had she said, "them"? My question had been singular, not plural. I wondered, but I let it pass.

Classic migraines have two phases. The first phase is thought to be caused by constriction of specific blood vessels supplying visual areas of the brain. This vasoconstriction causes the visual symptoms, the most common of which is bright jagged lines like lightning or shooting stars flashing in front of the patient. Phase two is due to sudden dilation or stretching of blood vessels and consists of severe, intense, throbbing pain accompanied by other signs and symptoms such as nausea, pallor, sweating, prostration, and lethargy. The pain is thought to be from the expansion and stretching of pain-sensitive blood vessels.

Mrs. Lockman fit the bill. She'd had a brief phase of bright flashing lights (called "scintillating scotomata" followed by a severe, intense, throbbing headache associated with generalized symptoms.

There were a few problems, however. I could *imagine* a migraine headache being precipitated by the various physiological and chemical changes that occur at the time of orgasm, but I'd neither read about such an occurrence nor seen such a patient. And Dr. Jansen was right that neurology taught that the sudden onset of a severe headache during active intercourse was a sign of bleeding from a weakened abnormal blood vessel. This was especially true for "the worst headache" of one's life. The headaches in such instances often have many of the characteristics of migraines. Jim Hearn's had, and he had bled from a small aneurysm or blister on a blood vessel going to his brain.

The sudden increase in blood pressure that occurs during orgasm was too much for the thin wall of his aneurysm; it ruptured. Before we could do anything, it ruptured again, and Jim Hearn died.

I dearly wanted Mrs. Lockman to have a long history of migraines or to have had headaches like this before. Either would mean that nothing new was going on—or at least nothing catastrophic or potentially fatal—but instead merely a quick and intense physiological stimulus bringing out her tendency to develop migraines. She'd already denied such a history twice, and there was no reason for me to ask her a third time.

I took her into the examining room and insisted her husband wait in my office. After all, I wasn't going to examine him.

"Four," she said. "This has happened to me four times before."

"What?"

"I've had headaches like this before, four times."

"Why didn't you tell me?"

"I couldn't tell Walt. He wouldn't understand." She hesitated before explaining what she meant. I was her doctor, and she'd come to me because of the headache, but she was more than just a little frightened. She then continued. "It happens whenever I have that intense an orgasm."

"Oh," I observed.

The first time had been five or six years earlier, the first time she'd ever made love in an airplane. The other three had happened in the past two years. All three times with the same man. That man was not her present husband but another psychiatrist, Clint Hartung, who she was going out with when she met Walt. For a while she'd gone out with both of them. Lovemaking with Clint Hartung was more intense physically than it was with Walter Lockman. But she loved Walt and Clint was a real bastard, so she decided to marry Walt.

The previous two headaches had followed encounters with Clint Hartung after she and Walt had become officially engaged. Both were the outcome of hurried couplings with very intense orgasms.

Had all five headaches been identical?

Yes.

Two phases?

Yes. The stars, then the headaches.

Did she ever get stars without the headaches?

She did.

How often?

Whenever it really worked.

I didn't ask her how often that was. It was none of my business.

But her past history was. The fact that this had happened before, a number of times over a number of years, changed the perspective radically. It meant that there was nothing for any of us to worry about, neurologically speaking. For years, her most intense orgasms, those with the most sudden and intense physiological components, had caused full-blown migraines. Others less dramatic caused just the first phase of a migraine, or a migraine equivalent.

Why only sometimes? Why not with each orgasm? That had to do with factors that were not neurological. But I asked her, and she knew. It happened whenever she really let go. She wanted to be able to do that all the time, but the pain was too great. Was there any way I could help her?, she wanted to know.

There was. First I explained to her exactly what the problem was. She could tell her husband as much or as little as she desired. I also put her on propanolol hydrochloride (Inderal) which is often able to prevent migraines by making the blood vessels less likely to suddenly dilate and cause pain. I told her husband it was just a simple migraine; no sudden bleeding, no aneurysm, nothing to worry about. I heard from both of them at Christmas time. They each sent me a Christmas card with a brief note.

Hers said, " I have had no more headaches, but I see stars at least twice a week. Astronomy is so much fun."

His said, "Many thanks. I may have to buy a new couch."

The first time I saw the second patient in the triumvirate, Lesley Westrum, was the very next afternoon. Hers was not an emergency consultation due to an acute episode. She had had the problem for years and had set up this neurological evaluation a month earlier. Forty-one and single, Ms. Westrum worked as a secretary. Migraines ran in her family—her mother had had them, as did one of her two brothers—and she had had migraines since her teens. They were classic migraine attacks: scintillating flashes of bright lights followed half an hour later by throbbing pain over one-half of her head. These were no big problem—they occurred only once or twice a year, and when they did, she took some Empirin with codeine and went to sleep. When she woke up, the headache was gone.

Why then had she come to see me? She got the headaches whenever she had sex. Her episodes were similar to her usual migraines, and very similar to the episodes that occurred to Carol Lockman. Sex was accompanied by one or two streaks of light in front of her right eye and then almost immediately by the sudden onset of crushing, throbbing pain beginning just behind the right eye and rapidly spreading to the entire right side of her head. It was as if her head were going to explode. It lasted about an hour to an hour and a half. There was no feeling of nausea and no vomiting.

When had it first happened?

In her early twenties.

Did it happen every time she had intercourse?

No, only if she had a climax.

Her neurological exam was normal. That did not surprise either of us. She was not particularly worried that she had any serious disease, for she'd had the problem for almost twenty years. She had seen another neurologist, who had done all sorts of tests and found absolutely nothing. She'd had a normal EEG and even a normal spinal tap and a normal CAT scan. She'd come to me to see whether there was anything I could do to help her.

That depended upon how much of a problem it was.

She understood exactly what I meant. "Once or twice a month," she told me. She felt that that was too infrequent to justify taking Inderal or any other medicine she'd have to take three times a day, seven days a week.

Did she know when?

Yes, on weekends.

Could she tell a half hour or so before that she would be at risk?

Yes.

What sort of birth control did she use?

A diaphragm.

That was perfect. I gave her a sample of Bellergal, a mild antimigranous medication that sometimes prevents the onset of migraine. I gave her twelve and instructed her to keep them with her diaphragm and to take two whenever she inserted her diaphragm.

She called me back in two weeks.

It had worked wonderfully. But . . . she was out of Bellergal already.

I sent her a prescription for sixty with three refills.

Two such patients in two days. Was it a coincidence? Or had benign headaches associated with orgasms become an epidemic? As far as I knew, it was not a well-known disorder. I went to the library to learn what I could. There wasn't much.

The occurrence of an apparently benign form of sexual headache was first reported in 1970 in a series of twenty-five Czechoslovakian patients. The paper was written in Czech, and I, like most other neurologists in America in 1972, was unaware that anyone had seriously studied this problem. Most of the patients the Czech author studied were men who suffered severe debilitating headache associated with sexual activity. The neurological examination had been normal for every patient, and the author concluded that the headaches were associated with the increase in blood pressure induced by the stress and physical exertion associated with sexual activity.

In 1969 Jim Lance, an Australian neurologist, had published a well-known monograph on headache. In it he included some anecdotal reports of patients with apparently benign headaches precipitated by coitus. Nevertheless, in 1972 benign sexual headache was still not well recognized as a distinct phenomenon, at least not in the English-language literature. In fact, the editors at the *British Medical Journal* had just recently responded to a question about headaches associated with orgasm in a fifty-year-old female by stating that this was "not a recognized phenomenon." In response to this, a number of anecdotal reports of apparently benign coital headaches were sent to the *BMJ*. One told of six cases of benign headache associated with coitus. All six patients were males who reported recurrent severe headaches toward the end of intercourse. The headaches were bilateral in most instances, predominantly occipital (posterior), and lasted from ten minutes to one hour. Half of the patients had a past history of migraines.

At the time I saw my two patients, most neurologists faced with a patient who developed a severe headache during intercourse would immediately have considered the sudden rupture or expansion of either a vascular malformation or an aneurysm to be the most likely culprit, although few such patients are reported in the literature. C. Miller Fisher published the history of one such patient with a ruptured carotid artery aneurysm who gave a history of severe headaches during intercourse on six occasions in the six months before the rupture of the aneurysm. In this paper Miller mentioned another patient with orgasmic pain who probably had an intracerebral hemorrhage, and commented briefly on other patients with pain of uncertain cause during intercourse. Fisher suggested that the pain produced by intercourse results from a temporary rise in systemic blood pressure, which stretches the aneurysmal sac. Headaches of a similar nature can be brought about by lifting or strain, probably through a similar mechanism.

Following the Rule of Three, I saw a third patient with similar, and similarly precipitated, symptoms, this one a male, Don Mueller. The thirty-three-year-old high school teacher had been hospitalized because of his severe headache, and I was asked to see him as an emergency consultation. When I entered his room, he was lying perfectly flat, with no pillow at all. The lights were on. His radio was blaring away. Neither the lights nor the noise bothered him at all.

His headache was a severe bilateral throbbing involving the entire back of his head. It had been precipitated by intercourse and had begun immediately with orgasm. It was relieved by resting in a supine position but returned when he stood up. He had had one previous headache similar to this at age thirty-one. It had been identical in nature but less severe than it was this time. He had stayed in bed for two days with the first episode and then was able to go to work despite some mild residual throbbing. This second episode of severe headache had resulted in hospitalization. Don had no past history of migraine headache, no family history of migraine, no history of significant psychiatric disease or any significant illness at all. His general physical examination and his neurological examination were normal. So were his skull x-rays and his EEG. The resident had already done a lumbar puncture. The opening pressure was less than 10 mm, but everything else was entirely normal.

It was obvious that Don Mueller's headache was different from Carol Lockman's and Lesley Westrum's. While his, like theirs, had been precipitated by sexual intercourse, the resemblance ended there. Their headaches had been classic migraines, but his were not. His headache began with no first-phase aura and, uncharacteristically of a migraine, was relieved by lying supine and exacerbated by any elevation of his head. This phenomenon was well known to me and all neurologists. It's what happens to patients who develop headaches following lumbar puncture. It was my hypothesis that Don Mueller's headache was in fact just that—a position-sensitive headache due to a spontaneous rupture of the covering of the spinal fluid space.

When we do a spinal tap, the pressure in the fluid is almost always above 60 mm. His had been below that—far below that. Such extremely low spinal fluid pressure had been proposed to be the basic cause of the headaches that are seen after lumbar punctures. And this low pressure is thought to be due to continued leakage of spinal fluid through the iatrogenic defect

caused by puncturing the coverings of the spinal fluid space
with a needle. In Mr. Mueller I thought that it was quite possible that a rent in the spinal fluid space occurred during the
physiological stress of coitus. The relation of posture to pain
was identical to that seen in patients with headache following
lumbar puncture. Whenever they stand up, the pressure of the
fluid within the spinal canal increases, forcing more fluid out
of the hole and resulting in a sudden drop in pressure and the
subsequent severe headache.

If that was the case, continued bed rest should allow the hole
to repair itself, and he should be cured. I advised him to lie flat
in bed as much as possible. Within one week his headaches
disappeared and he returned to work. He returned to active
sexual behavior within one month, and the last I heard, he had
experienced no recurrence of headache in eight years.

Several weeks later I discussed these three patients with a
colleague of mine from Ohio State University named George
Paulson. He too had seen such patients—not three in a week,
but eight or ten in the last couple of years. We decided to pool
our experiences and publish a paper on the subject so that
other neurologists would be aware that headaches caused by
coitus could be a benign disease. We entitled our paper "Benign
Orgasmic Cephalgia." All told we collected fourteen patients.

Why had this hitherto unknown phenomenon become so
common that we were able to collect so many patients in a
rather short time? Quite possibly it was because the so-called
sexual revolution had resulted in greater candor regarding the
symptoms associated with sexual activity. It's unlikely that this
was really a new disease. Of the fourteen patients we collected,
the majority were women ranging from twenty to sixty years
old. In all cases, the headaches had been associated with orgasm, not just sexual activity per se. In no case was any underlying psychopathological factor considered to be significant.
Overall, George and I divided our patients into two groups in
which we believed distinctly different pathophysiological
mechanisms were at work. In the larger group (eleven patients,
including Carol Lockman and Lesley Westrum), a vascular

mechanism analogous to migraine was thought to underlie the headaches. In the remaining three patients (including Don Mueller), we thought lowered cerebrospinal fluid pressure analogous to postlumbar puncture headache was the cause.

Eight years later, my oldest daughter took a course in neuropsychology at Northwestern. The professor recognized her name.

"Klawans," he said. "Are you related to Harold Klawans, the neurologist?"

"Yes," she said promptly, beaming. She knew I was well known for my work on Parkinson's disease, Huntington's chorea, and Tourette's syndrome.

"He's famous," her professor continued. "He was the first person to describe headaches caused by orgasms."

Such is fame.

AUTHOR'S NOTE

The original article "Benign Orgasmic Cephalgia" by Paulson and Klawans appeared in *Headache* (13: 181–87, 1974). The most comprehensive review of the entire subject is:

Braun, A. and H. L. Klawans. "Headaches associated with exercise and sexual activity." *Handbook of Clinical Neurology,* ed. P. J. Vinken, G. W. Bruyn, and H. L. Klawans, Vol. 48, 373–82. Amsterdam: Elsevier, 1986.

14

The Hounds of Hell

A hound it was, an enormous coal-black hound, but not such a hound as mortal eyes have ever seen. Fire burst from its open mouth, its eyes glowed with a smouldering glare, its muzzle and hackles and dewlap were outlined in flickering flame. Never in the delirious dream of a disordered brain could anything more savage, more appalling, more hellish be conceived than that dark form and savage face which broke upon us out of the wall of fog.
A. Conan Doyle, *The Hound of the Baskervilles* (1901, 1902)

I should have recognized him as I walked through my waiting room to get to the receptionist's desk on that day in 1978. I always use that brief exposure to observe my patients in a more natural setting than my office or examining room. So I observed him but didn't recognize him, although I'd seen him once about a year before for a relatively minor neurological problem. And while I'm not terribly good at remembering names, I rarely forget a neurological history and the face that goes with it.

I picked up the next chart and called his name: "Risberg. Charles Risberg."

As he turned toward me, I was surprised that this person had an appointment with me. He was unshaven, slovenly even. I'd assumed he was one of the alcoholics being seen by the residents in their clinic.

I watched his every move, my neurological examination already beginning. "Mr. Risberg," I said, nodding my head in the direction of the suite of examining rooms.

He smiled at me, with as controlled a smile as I had ever seen. Was that because his facial muscles were weak? Or because he had parkinsonism? Or something else?

The smile was symmetrical, being equally limited on both sides of his face, a minor movement that was less a smile than a mere sign of recognition. The symmetry of the muscle movements made weakness of facial muscles an unlikely cause. Several diseases can cause weakness of both sides of the face with accompanying wan smiles, but those smiles are rarely completely symmetrical. One side of the face is almost invariably weaker, more abnormal, and therefore moves less when the person smiles. If, as in this case, the excursions of the two sides of the face are equally restricted, it's more likely to be due to Parkinson's disease.

I nodded toward the examining room a second time and took a step in that direction. My eyes were still riveted on Mr. Risberg. Parkinsonism, I was thinking. Yet there was something wrong, something about his face that wasn't right. He hadn't shaved in more than a week. He had what would be called a salt-and-pepper beard on a man with more class and a larger bank account.

Mr. Risberg bounced straight up from the chair, and in six long, confident strides was standing at the doorway to the examining room area. So much for a diagnosis of parkinsonism. He had absolutely no signs of slowness in initiating movements, which is typical of parkinsonism. No shortstop in the prime of life had ever moved more fluidly. Whatever was wrong with his face was not caused by Parkinson's disease. I needed a new hypothesis.

I led him into an examining room, had him sit on the examining table, and sat opposite him. It was more like two or three weeks that he'd gone without shaving. Perhaps he'd decided to grow a beard, especially on the left side. But that couldn't be right—no disheveled alcoholic I had ever seen had been asymmetrically slovenly. In fact, no one I'd ever known had intentionally grown a beard that was longer on one side of his face than the other.

I also observed that his collar did not fit him. His shirt was at least a size too big for his neck, yet it was not old and frazzled. This was not a businessman who had fallen on bad times and was wearing clothes he should have discarded years ago. It was this year's shirt, bearing a designer's name, Alexander Julian. My son had given me the same shirt for my birthday—but not with the matching silk tie Mr. Risberg wore. Those two items had cost well over a hundred dollars. So no hard times, at least not economically.

I introduced myself.

He nodded vigorously and said softly, "I met you last year." I remembered. He was a bank president, or at least he had been, and of a rather substantial bank at that. And he never drank.

"Mr. Risberg," I said in as friendly a tone as I could muster, "I remember."

Now he said his words softly. Yet the articulation of each word and the flow of his speech were normal. I was certain that the loss of volume was not due to any neurological deficit. He never once moved his jaws while he spoke. He moved his lips hardly at all and only up and down, never horizontally. The idea of a broken jaw sprang into my mind.

That was it, I thought. He had broken his jaw, and it was wired together. That would explain the lack of jaw movements when he talked. And the weight loss—it was not the Alexander Julian shirt and matching tie that were too large, it was the neck that had become too small. But a broken jaw could not account for the lack of shaving or the failure to move his facial muscles when he smiled or talked.

"You've lost weight," I observed.

"Twenty-seven pounds," he said, again with as little movement of his face as possible.

"Did you break your jaw?"

"No," he said. The contrast between the essentially minimal movement of his jaws and face and the vigorous shaking of his head had me at a loss.

It was time to quit guessing. "Tell me, Mr. Risberg," I began, "what brings you back to see me again?"

"My face."

"Tell me the story from the beginning."

He did. Once again he was the precise, articulate, observant patient that I now vividly recalled. It had begun so suddenly, in such a brief flash, that he hadn't even known it had begun. It was an ordinary Tuesday morning. He'd just finished shaving and was cleaning the traces of shaving cream from his face with a hot washcloth when a jolt, like a jolt of lightning, shot across his left jaw. And then it was gone. Before he could react, almost before it began, it had disappeared.

Had it lasted a second?

He doubted it. It was an instantaneous, intense, white-hot streak, too brief to be called painful. Then he rubbed his face again, gingerly at first. Nothing happened. Then he rubbed vigorously. Still nothing happened.

He thought nothing of it, continued getting dressed, and went to work. Someone was interested in buying his bank, and the final negotiations were about to begin. It was an opportunity of a lifetime for him if he could get what he really wanted. He would have more money than he'd ever dreamed of and he'd still be president of the bank.

Two days later, it hit him again. The same, only different. He was at lunch with the prospective buyers.

Had he touched his face?

He wasn't sure. Once again it was a sudden flash, a white-hot, intensely painful jolt. But this one was not over before it began. It lasted much longer than an instant. An eternity, he said.

"How long did it last?" I asked.

"Less than a minute."

The pain had been excruciating, the worst pain he had ever felt. Far worse than the sciatic pain he'd suffered ten years ago or anything any dentist had ever subjected him to. Then it stopped, as quickly as it had started. The luncheon and the negotiations went on.

He hoped to God it wouldn't come back. But it did. That night at home, while he was eating dinner it came back, not once, but twice. Searing, sharp, awful pains cutting across the left side of his face that lasted less than a minute but seemed to last a lifetime. Each had started while he was chewing, so he stopped chewing. He had not really eaten a meal since that day. He'd kill for a good meal without that pain, even for a meal at

McDonald's, but eating wasn't worth those pains.

The next day Mr. Risberg went to see his dentist, who announced proudly that he'd found the problem. Two of Mr. Risberg's crowns on the left didn't fit quite right, and there was some erosion beneath them. The balance of his jaws was off, and his bite was all wrong.

His dentist went to work, but the pains continued. They became more frequent, now occurring every single day, and not just once or twice each day, but five or ten times. Often even more than that—a dozen, two dozen times a day. He couldn't eat anything he had to chew, for fear that the movement of his jaw would precipitate yet another horrid jolt. He was even afraid to wash his face.

The dentist went to work at a feverish pace, and he was done in two weeks. Mr. Risberg's teeth and jaw were now perfect; there was no malclosure and no abnormality of alignment. The dentist was satisfied. His patient no longer had any reason at all for any pain.

But Mr. Risberg still had the pains. By then he'd lost eight pounds and acquired a large dental bill.

The dentist sent him to an oral surgeon, who found nothing. But every time he forced Mr. Risberg's jaw open to probe the back of his mouth, the pain was excruciating.

An endodontist was the next stop. According to him, Mr. Risberg needed to have two root canals cleaned out. Four visits and another week and a half later, the endodontist pronounced him free of dental disease—as had his dentist and the oral surgeon. He went to another endodontist, and even a periodontist. Perhaps, he was told, he should see another oral surgeon.

And still not an hour went by during any day when the pain did not strike him at least once. Now the pain had begun to awaken him at night. He had lost almost twenty pounds by then. He gave up shaving on the left side. He stopped going to work.

He went to see his internist. His internist was alarmed by the weight loss and ordered tests—blood tests, x-rays, EKGs. They were all normal.

This once rugged, powerful fifty-eight-year-old bank president was now haggard and beaten, a shadow of what he had been only two months before. His internist suggested a psychiatrist, thinking it had to be the pressure of the negotiations. Mr. Risberg knew that that was not the solution.

That was last week, April 8. While working, on his income tax, he saw my bill from the earlier treatment and thought perhaps I could help him again.

I knew that I could. I asked him to describe the pain to me as well as he could.

"It's as if all of the hounds of hell have been set loose at once and are tearing at my face."

While graphic, and literary, that was not what I needed. Where was the pain?

On the left side of his face.

Where precisely?

The lower jaw and lower part of his face.

Did it ever cross over to the right?

He thought hard before he replied. No, never.

And the precise character of the pain? This was a harder question. Patients are usually much better at telling precisely where the pain is than in coming up with words to tell exactly what the pain is like, in part because our vocabulary is not developed to describe our own pain.

But he did not hesitate at all. He knew the right words: sharp, shooting, lightning-like, like the worst electric shock imaginable. Only worse.

What brings it on?

What doesn't?

What I needed were examples. I asked him to list them.

Touching his face.

Where?

On the left. Especially near his lower lip.

Where else?

Chewing, opening his jaw, any jaw movement. Eating—not swallowing, but eating. And yawning—that was a torment beyond belief. And brushing his teeth—the Chinese water torture was, he was certain, child's play in comparison.

I asked him to open his jaw. He did, slowly and cautiously. Then he suddenly stopped with his jaw only partially opened. He froze in midmovement. His face became contorted as if he was in agony. His eyes opened wide. His entire body became tense as if any further motion would bring on a catastrophe of cosmic proportions.

I timed it. It lasted no more than twelve seconds. "Was that your usual pain?"

"Yes," he whispered, as motionlessly as possible, his face as masklike as that of any patient I'd ever seen with Parkinson's disease.

"How long do you think it lasted?"

"A minute. A lifetime. Far too long. I'm not crazy. Help me."

"No, you're not crazy. And I can help you."

Mr. Charles Risberg did have a neurological disease. It's called *tic douloureux* or *trigeminal neuralgia*, neuralgia of the trigeminal nerve. The trigeminal nerve is one of the twelve pairs of cranial nerves that extend from the brain to the various parts of the head, face, and neck. These nerves carry out either special functions such as smell, taste, hearing, or sight, or general functions such as touch or movement, the same kinds of functions that other nerves perform elsewhere in the body. We each have two trigeminal nerves. Each of these nerves supplies sensation to half of the face—the left trigeminal nerve to the left side, the right to the right. And each stops at the midline.

Mr. Risberg's pain stopped at the midline. His pain was restricted to the areas of his left trigeminal nerve, and his nerve went just where it should. Each trigeminal nerve has three branches. One goes to the forehead, one to the cheek and upper jaw, one to the lower part of the face, lower jaw, and gums over the lower jaw. Mr. Risberg's pain followed the course of the third division of his left trigeminal nerve. This is neuralgia of the third division of the fifth cranial nerve—the trigeminal nerve—hence trigeminal neuralgia.

Like the other general nerves of the body, the trigeminal nerve carries all kinds of sensations from the face to the brain:

pain, touch, pressure, position sense, temperature. Each of these is carried along separate fibers within the nerve. Once they enter the brain, the fibers separate and travel along separate pathways to get to different final destinations. But in the nerve itself, they are intermixed and travel together. That anatomical fact explained Mr. Risberg's entire clinical problem.

The cause of trigeminal neuralgia has perplexed neurologists for years. Dr. Henry Head, who was the leading English neurologist at the turn of the century and was editor in chief of the prestigious English neurology journal *Brain*, made a particular study of this disease. He examined the ganglion of a trigeminal nerve that had been removed by Sir Victor Horsley, the founding father of neurosurgery, from a patient with trigeminal neuralgia. The ganglion is that part of the nerve where the cell bodies of each nerve cell are grouped together. Head spent many months sectioning and examining the ganglion under the microscope. When he was done, his preparations were used by a medical school as an example of normal histologic sections of the fifth nerve. Head had found absolutely nothing wrong in the ganglion of the nerve that had caused such horrible pain. He had unfortunately looked in the wrong place.

Today we understand the mechanism behind trigeminal neuralgia somewhat better. And the key to our understanding is the way in which these pains can be triggered.

Most patients with trigeminal neuralgia tell you just what Mr. Risberg told me. The pains are seldom completely spontaneous. Some movement of the face, jaw, or tongue produces immediate paroxysms of intolerable pain. To avoid the pain, the patient cannot eat, talk, spit, or curse. He cannot even pray to God to relieve him of the pain—at least not out loud. Washing his face and shaving become intolerable. The patient will point to areas where these paroxysms are more likely to arise but does not want to touch that area. Mr. Risberg pointed to the area adjacent to his lower lip; he hadn't touched it. We call these areas "trigger zones." When someone or something touches a trigger zone, that sensation of touch travels up one of the thick nerve fibers of the trigeminal nerve into the brainstem, where it then travels through the pathways dedicated to the sensation of touch and reaches the brain proper. In Mr. Risberg these benign sensations of touch had crossed over into the wrong pathway and become transformed into pain.

How? Each of the nerve fibers, or axons, is covered by concentric layers of a fatty substance called *myelin*. The fats and proteins that make up these layers are not produced by the individual nerves themselves but by the supporting cells called the Schwann cells, which wrap themselves around the individual axons over and over again. It is this wrapping by layers of membrane of the Schwann cells that creates the myelin.

The myelin serves two purposes. First, the nerve fibers are specialized to transport electrical messages, and myelin speeds that process. Myelin also insulates the individual fibers from each other as the nerve fibers, or axons, travel together. Each axon is sensitive to electrical stimulation and must be insulated so that it is not triggered by the electrical impulses cascading through any of its neighbors. Because of this insulation, the electrical impulse traveling along a normal touch fiber to get to the touch pathways does not cross over into the pain fibers. And vice versa.

But if the myelin is lost or injured in a pain fiber, then the electrical impulse in the touch fiber can cross into a pain axon and trigger that axon. And if that axon is fired and carries its message to the brain, the brain recognizes that message as pain—sharp, shooting, lightning-like, electrical pain.

So if the insulation fails, touch can become pain. Each touch, for washing or shaving, can initiate an electric impulse that reaches the brain as excruciating pain. Pressure, the pressure of chewing a piece of meat or even a spoonful of mashed potatoes, becomes pain as well.

Position sense also becomes pain. These unconscious impulses keep the brain informed about where the parts of our body are at any moment. Every time we move, messages about the position of each part that has moved are sent to the brain, and these unconscious messages are generated in the receptors of each muscle. In the case of jaw movements, they begin in the jaw muscles and are sent up the trigeminal nerve toward the brain. But if such a message reaches the area where the insulation is not sufficient, the unconscious becomes conscious, and locations becomes pain as well. A yawn becomes intolerable, and opening the mouth is a torment.

Marked changes in temperature can also be converted into pain. Drinking a cold drink or a hot cup of coffee may also cause an attack.

That's the process, a process we couldn't understand at the turn of the century before telephones and telephone lines. For a nerve is much like a telephone line, composed of individual lines of communication coming from different locations and going to different locations but traveling together and protected from each other by insulation. When that insulation fails, the information coming over one telephone line is heard on the adjacent line, and you have crosstalk. In telecommunications it's merely aggravating. In the trigeminal nerve it's agonizing.

Sir Henry Head had studied the wrong part of the trigeminal nerve. He'd studied the ganglion, the collection of nerve-cell bodies that make up the trigeminal nerve. It was a natural mistake. After all, Sir Henry Head had probably never made a phone call to Sir Victor Horsley on an old trunk line whose insulation had worn out; he didn't know about crosstalk. The ganglion was the natural place for him to look. At that time neurologists tended to localize all disease in the cell bodies, not the axons, for axons merely carry the message. But in trigeminal neuralgia, the message *is* the disease.

I told Mr. Risberg that he had trigeminal neuralgia, and explained the nature of his problem to him, and told how I could help. I could not go in and replace the missing insulation, but I could give him medicine that would make crosstalk less likely by making the nerve fibers less sensitive to electrical stimulation. I prescribed an anticonvulsant called Tegretol or carbemazepine. I told him about its side effects, but I doubt he bothered to listen.

In two weeks he was pain-free. Two weeks after that he completed the negotiations to his satisfaction. He remained as chief executive officer and had a lot more money in the bank. When I saw him a month later, he was clean-shaven and had regained eight pounds. He was wearing a different Alexander Julian shirt, and it fit him perfectly. He asked me how he'd gotten trigeminal neuralgia.

I wasn't sure. It wasn't due to a virus, I told him, or any other specific disease. The loss of myelin is usually the result of pressure on the nerve itself. As we age, we lose brain cells and our brain shrinks a bit. That shrinkage increases the distance that each of the nerves must travel to get from the brain to the various holes in the base of the skull by which they exit the cranial cavity. The nerves don't get any longer, so this increase in distance increases the tension on the nerves as they travel away from the brain. This often pulls them against various other structures, such as the bones of the skull or veins or arteries. The resulting pressure of these abnormal contacts can cause a disruption of the myelin and, with it, crosstalk.

Mr. Risberg seemed dissatisfied with this explanation.

I reminded him of his other neurological problem. He'd come in the year before complaining of numbness and tingling in his left hand. He'd had a mild compression of the nerve going through his wrist into his hand, due to injury to the wrist itself. The door on his shower stall stuck, and each morning he banged it open by striking it with the inside of his left wrist: self-inflicted trauma.

At that time, to convince him that the wrist was the source of his previous problem, I'd tapped his wrist firmly with my rubber hammer. That tap had caused a sharp shooting pain into his palm. Pressure had become pain: crosstalk, due to pressure. I'd told him to stop slamming his wrist into his shower door and his numbness would resolve. He had the door fixed and did as I told him, and the numbness did as I predicted.

I now turned his hand over and struck him with my rubber hammer. He felt the pressure but no shooting pain. The pressure in his wrist had receded. The nerve had repaired itself.

Would the trigeminal nerve repair itself? Perhaps.

He called me when he'd been pain-free for three months. I withdrew his Tegretal slowly over a month. His pain did not come back. It still might, but if it does, we can always restart the Tegretal.

That was two years ago. As far as I know, the pain has not come back. Mr. Risberg is still president of the same bank. His life has changed only in minor ways. He has a new dentist and a new internist.

AUTHOR'S NOTE

The use of anticonvulsants in the treatment of trigeminal neuralgia stems from the work reported in:

Iannone A., Baker A. B., and Morrell F. "Dilantin in the treatment of neuralgia." *Neurology* 8: 126–28 (1958).

This treatment is based upon the ability of anticonvulsants to act as "membrane stabilizers" and as such to combat crosstalk. For a review of the other possible mechanisms involved in trigeminal neuralgia, see:

Fields N., and Raskin, N. "Anticonvulsants and pain." *Clinical Neuropharmacology* 1: 173–85 (1976).

Sir Henry Head may not have understood the anatomical basis of trigeminal neuralgia, but he did make numerous important contributions to neurology. He answered one particularly thorny question: What is the distribution of the different sensory nerves? That is, which nerve goes to which part of the body? This is almost impossible to answer. A live person cannot tell which of his nerves is diseased. A dead patient cannot tell you which part of his body was innervated by any specific diseased nerve. A true conundrum, and more than merely a philosophical issue.

But Henry Head knew how to solve it: by studying shingles. Shingles is a viral disease called *Herpes zoster*. Caused by the same virus that causes chicken pox, *Herpes zoster* is due to the presence of the virus in one specific nerve root. It causes pain in that nerve root and a rash in the skin served by that nerve.

If one saw enough cases of *Herpes zoster*, one would eventually see cases in which every nerve root was involved. And if one carefully outlined the distribution of the shingles in each case and put them all together, one would have a map of the sensory innervation of the entire body. That's what Henry Head did, dashing around the English countryside in the years before World War I.

Henry Head was not the only neurologist who tried to answer the question. Otfrid Foerster had a different solution. If Henry Head represented the flower of English neurology, Foerster was the leading German neurologist. Also in the years just before World War I, at the age of forty, Foerster began to practice neurosurgery. At heart he was neither a neurologist nor a neurosurgeon but an experimental neurophysiologist. He would help his patients if he could, but they had to pay the price of being subjected to his own physiological experimentation. And experiment he did.

He too wanted to know where each nerve root went—he had to know.

But how? No single part of the skin was innervated by just one nerve, so to Foerster the maps of Henry Head had too much overlap—not neat enough. Foerster was certain that he could get a neater, more reliable answer by operating on patients and cutting two or three consecutive nerve roots, thereby leaving part of their bodies without sensation. Then he could map out the lower level of the root above those he had cut and the upper level of the root below. With enough patients, he too could draw a map.

That's what he did. There was rarely, if ever, a medical reason to cut the roots, but that never stopped him.

His map was no different from Henry Head's, no neater or more precise. The difference between the two approaches has always struck me as more than the difference between two men. Was it not in part the differences in their cultures? Or am I prejudiced? Foerster did not reject either the honor or the administrative roles given him by the Third Reich in the 1930s. Why should he have? Was his philosophy any different from theirs? Or am I too harsh? I think not.

I once heard a lecture by an American neurologist who had studied with Foerster in the twenties. This man tearfully lamented Foerster's involvement with the Nazis and wondered how such a brilliant man could have sunk so far.

But I was not certain he had sunk at all. I doubt that any patient who had been unknowingly converted into an experimental subject had any difficulty understanding Foerster's behavior.

15
Broca's Amusica

When I met Lynn Rowe at a wedding in 1986, her nervous system was, I'm told, functioning entirely normally and had been for several years. The meeting had been set up by the bride, Ms. Kris Gehringer, soon to become Dr. Kris Gehringer, the wife of Dr. Michael Cochrane. The bride had been a student of mine. She was going into psychiatry and felt that she should have a better background in neurology than most medical students, so she spent an extra four weeks studying with me, for I had the good fortune to be the attending physician who made teaching rounds each day that month.

It was during these last four weeks that Kris told me about Lynn Rowe. She and Lynn had gone to college together and had both started out as music majors. Kris played the violin, Lynn the oboe. They had both ended up as premeds—Kris because she liked science and just wasn't that good a musician, Lynn because she woke up one morning and discovered that she could no longer play her oboe. Otherwise she was absolutely normal.

She could walk and talk and read and write. She could even read music. But she could not make a single note come out of her oboe. She didn't even know how to hold the oboe anymore. She had no idea where to put her fingers. She couldn't blow a single note, much less produce a melody. So ended the promising musical career of Lynn Rowe, who had been the most talented musician in their class—until that fateful morning.

Kris had not told me that story out of the blue. We had been discussing a patient with aphasia, the loss of the ability to use language. We'd gone over my five-step simple guideline to understanding aphasia:

First, aphasia is a loss of the use of language.

Second, aphasia is always due to a lesion of the dominant hemisphere for speech. In right-handed individuals this is always the left hemisphere. In left-handers the left hemisphere still usually is dominant for speech.

Third, if the patient has more trouble producing words than understanding them, the problem is located toward the front of the dominant hemisphere. The term *Broca's aphasia* or *expressive aphasia* is used to denote an aphasic state in which expression is more involved than comprehension. A patient with Broca's aphasia can understand relatively well. He can follow commands, even complicated ones, but he cannot really speak. His speech consists of a few syllables or words, and he cannot name objects correctly. The right words evade him. Pierre Broca (1824–1880) was not the first physician to describe such a patient, but his name became attached to this type of aphasia because he was the first one to associate it with a lesion in a specific location of the brain, namely the third frontal convolution on the left, a location now known as Broca's area.

Fourth, if the patient can produce speech fluently but cannot understand what is said to him and cannot follow commands, he has a lesion farther back in his brain. This is called a *receptive aphasia* or *Wernicke's aphasia*, named after Wernicke, a neurologist who did for receptive aphasia what Broca did for expressive aphasia.

And fifth, all the rest is mere commentary. Neurologists have described dozens of minor variations of these speech disorders. International experts have compiled lists of dozens of different variants and syndromes. No two use the same classification. No two agree about which ones are separate disorders, or about which names to use. It makes no difference to most of us, or to most of our patients. In essence, there are three rules:

1. Aphasia is a disorder of the dominant hemisphere.
2. Expressive aphasia is toward the front.
3. Receptive aphasia is toward the back.

Kris had seen and examined a patient with expressive aphasia and had told me the patient's history and described the examination results. We discussed aphasia, and then we went into the patient's room to examine him.

I knew he was in his sixties and his name was Mike Kreevich. I asked him his name.

He said nothing.

I introduced myself.

He looked at me alertly but made no response.

"How are you?" I asked.

"Fine," he said. A single word.

"Where are you?"

"Fine." A single word repeated when it no longer was appropriate.

"Who are you?"

"Fine." And repeated yet again.

I held out my watch and asked him what it was.

"Time." The wrong word. Close but no cigar.

I pointed to the watch band and asked my same question.

"Time," he repeated.

I waited and pointed to the stem.

I got no answer.

"What is this called?"

No reply.

"What do you do with this?" I asked, still pointing to the stem.

No response.

"Show me."

He did. He took the watch and rotated the stem.

In the end, I was able to demonstrate that Mr. Kreevich had all of the classic manifestations of a Broca's aphasia. His speech was subfluent, telegraphic. All he could say was a few words and occasional short phrases. He had a marked difficulty in naming simple objects. But he could follow complex commands and understand ideas.

This classic Broca's aphasia was caused by an acute stroke involving Broca's area or the tracts deep in the brain leading to and from Broca's area.

"What else can he do?" I asked. Kris didn't understand my question. "Can he sing?" I asked her.

She didn't know. She hadn't asked. Of course, she realized asking might not have helped.

I smiled. She was right—it was not a question one could ask him. Instead I began to sing. "Oh say can you see . . . ." I stopped. "Sing with me," I said, and started again. "Oh say can you see . . . ."

Mr. Kreevich began to sing with me. "By the dawn's early light . . . ."

I stopped.

He continued. "What so proudly we hailed . . . ." He was still singing as we left his room.

Kris immediately grasped the significance of what she had observed. The ability to sing was not lost in a Broca's aphasia. That meant that singing, although it involves words and language, did not pass through Broca's area. A lesion of Broca's area prevented expression of spoken language but not of singing. "Where is singing controlled?" she asked.

"The minor hemisphere," I replied. The minor hemisphere is also referred to as the nondominant hemisphere. In right-handers this is invariably the right hemisphere. In left-handers it is still usually the right hemisphere.

"How can you be sure?" she asked, good student that she was.

I told her about the few published cases of patients with acute amusica, the sudden loss of musical abilities. In these patients the amusica was due to disorders of the minor hemisphere. "Like aphasiacs," I said, "most patients with amusica have both expressive and receptive problems. And the same rules apply. The disease in expressive amusica is toward the front of the right hemisphere. In receptive, it's toward the back."

The look on her face changed. "Lynn," she said.

"Who?" I replied.

"If the lesion is toward the front," she began quite flatly, "the patient would have more trouble making music—or playing an instrument—than reading music, while if it's more toward the back of the brain, she'd have had more trouble reading music than playing it."

I nodded. She was absolutely correct. "And all the rest is mere commentary."

"No," she said. "That's not true."

Before I could ask her to explain her comment, she asked me a question. "Is there such a thing as a pure Broca's amusica?"

The term Broca's amusica did not exist. It contains inherent contradictions: Broca's aphasia refers to speech, not musical abilities, and Broca's area refers to the region that controls speech, not the ability to make music. But I understood what Kris meant. She wanted to know if there was a pure syndrome in which the comprehension of music was normal but the ability to make music, to play a musical instrument, was totally lost—the minor hemisphere's equivalent of a Broca's aphasia, a Broca's amusica, so to speak. It was as good a term as any I had ever heard. "Yes," I said.

"That's what happened to Lynn," she said. And then she told me the story.

She and Lynn had been juniors in college. Kris had already switched from music to premed. But Lynn was still planning on a career as a professional oboe player in a major symphony orchestra, and she had already had some offers. Then one morning Lynn had awakened feeling fine, gone to class, and been unable to play her oboe.

She could read music. She could copy music. She could write music. She could read the words in songs. But she could not sing them, and she could not play a single note on her oboe. Otherwise she was fine.

She went to the student health service, but she didn't think she was sick. Nor did they. They referred her to a psychiatrist, thinking it was obviously a psychiatric problem. After all, her boyfriend had just walked out on her, having decided that he was more interested in other men than he was in Lynn.

"She'd been so normal," Kris complained.

"And the sexual symbolism of the oboe was so obvious," I added.

"Yes."

Lynn had undergone extensive psychotherapy and had dropped out of school for two years. She got somewhat better, able to play simple tunes on her oboe. She went back to school as a premed and was now a first-year medical student.

"It wasn't a psychiatric problem," I said.

"Broca's amusica," she said. "But what would cause that?"

"Usually it's a stroke. And strokes in young women who are otherwise healthy. . . ." I paused.

"She was healthy. She still is."

"That leaves only two causes. The commonest is a complication of a migraine."

"She didn't have migraines."

"The other is a stroke due to use of birth-control pills."

Neither of us replied to that. After all, Lynn had not been in her own bed that morning.

Kris called Lynn and told her what we had hypothesized. It was hard for her to accept the news just like that. She had undergone years of analysis. Could I prove that was what had happened?

Kris and I discussed it. Kris called Lynn back and told her to get a CAT scan of her brain. If it showed evidence of an old stroke on her nondominant hemisphere, then the answer was obvious.

As we danced at Kris's wedding, Lynn told me about her CAT scan. It showed an old stroke.

"In the right hemisphere," I said.

"Yes."

"Where?"

"Opposite Broca's area," she said.

She then thanked me. At first the new diagnosis had made her angry. After all, her psychiatrist had made the wrong diagnosis. But he had helped her adjust to her inability to play her oboe no matter what the cause. Without that she might never have been able to shift gears so successfully. Kris was right. Lynn was well adjusted.

"Stop your pills," I said.

"I did," she said. "Years ago. Right after my . . . stroke. I was too depressed for sex, so I stopped taking them."

"Don't ever take them again," I said.

"I won't," she said. "Don't worry."

That is how the term *Broca's amusica* was first invented. Sometimes I'm tempted to call it Gehringer's amusica. After all, it was Kris Gehringer who recognized that Lynn Rowe's specific defect was an expressive amusica. And the CAT scan that she ordered demonstrated a stroke of the third frontal convolution on the right hemisphere—Gehringer's area.

But I call it Broca's amusica anyway. Somehow that term sounds better.

16
Mere Commentary

My family and I were in Israel for the summer. It was a sabbatical for me, and we were living in a small community called Neve Ilan. It's a moshav, or economic cooperative, located in the Judean Hills about ten kilometers outside of Jerusalem. It was the end of July. The days were warm, the evenings cool. I was spending most of the time working on a textbook I was writing, and my work was going smoothly.

Then I got a phone call from a lawyer in Illinois for whom I had acted as an expert witness in a lawsuit involving a number of railroad workers who had been exposed to dioxin. I had already testified for three days in early June, and I assumed he was calling to tell me that the trial was over and that the good guys had won. I was wrong. The trial was still going on, and he needed me to testify once again but in a different capacity, as a rebuttal witness. It would take only a day at the most.

My response was less than enthusiastic. I had no interest in leaving my home away from home to be cross-examined by a series of hostile lawyers in a courtroom in southern Illinois. Although I balked, I agreed to go.

The next Monday my sojourn began.

Tel Aviv to London.

London to Chicago.

A quick cab ride into the city to have dinner with my mother, then back to the airport.

Chicago to St. Louis.

Then a two-hour drive in a waiting limousine. I had arrived.

The lawyer and I worked most of the night going over the facts of the case, the testimony that had been given since I had been a witness seven weeks earlier, and the issues I would have to address in rebuttal. By five in the morning I thought we were ready. It was after lunchtime at Neve Ilan, and I was running down quickly. I figured I could sleep until noon since I was not scheduled to testify until one-thirty.

Wrong again. I'd come straight from Israel, where no one ever wore a summer suit, and the lawyer said I needed to testify in a suit to be a credible witness in the eyes of the twelve jurors. I needed a suit—and a tie, new wing-tip shoes, and a new shirt. To say nothing of a haircut. And it all had to be done by noon.

I let him make the arrangements. I tried to get some sleep, but it was impossible. I was used to sleeping on a hard Israeli bed with the cool night breezes of the Judean hills, not on an overly soft mattress in some stuffy air-conditioned plastic room. Besides, it was three o'clock in the afternoon, my time. I hadn't slept in over thirty hours, and was exhausted, but I'd never been able to sleep in the afternoon.

I tossed and turned for a couple of hours, and then a young lawyer knocked on my door. It was time to get started. My morning was full:

8:00—Shave and haircut.

8:45—Choosing the right suit.

9:30—First fitting at the tailors.

10:00—Accessories.

10:30—Shoes.

11:00—Second fitting.

11:30—Lunch meeting with the lawyer.

1:30—Appearance as a rebuttal expert witness.

The suit looked great, the shirt and tie matched it perfectly, the shoes, although a bit on the conservative side, fit the scene, and not a hair was out of place.

In my testimony, only two major issues had to be addressed. The lawyer asked me just two questions. I answered them in about two minutes apiece. That was our plan: Keep it short, sweet, and unambiguous. Then, when they cross-examined me for hours, the jury would remember the two succinct answers to the only two questions that mattered and not the hours of nit-picking.

But there was no nit-picking, no cross-examination at all. When I had testified originally, my three hours of direct testimony had been followed by three days of hostile cross-examination. Not this time. They asked me no questions.

It was 1:45 P.M. and I was done. It was bedtime at Neve Ilan. After the anticlimactic testimony, my adrenaline was still pumping me up, but I was exhausted.

The limousine was there to start the two-hour drive to the St. Louis airport. While we drove, someone in the lawyer's office made my travel arrangements and called my wife in Israel to tell her when I'd arrive.

A two-hour wait, pacing back and forth in the airport.

St. Louis to New York.

Another two-hour wait.

New York to Paris.

I tried to sleep but I couldn't. They served dinner. They sold cigarettes and perfume. They showed a movie. They finally turned off the lights, and then an hour later they served breakfast.

A four-hour wait at Charles DeGaulle Airport—not long enough to go into the city but too long to just relax and read a good book.

I hadn't slept in three nights, or was it four? Or two? I'd lost track.

Paris to Tel Aviv. Immigration. Customs. The cab stand. I expected to grab a cab to Neve Ilan. When my wife was there to pick me up, with our best friends from Neve Ilan, I knew I was in trouble.

They were all so glad that I'd gotten back so soon. They had a wonderful surprise. I didn't need a surprise. I needed my bed and the cool breezes of the Judean Hills. My new shirt was becoming fused to my skin.

"What's the surprise?" I asked hesitantly, afraid that the answer, no matter what it was, would delay my rendezvous with my bed.

It would. We all had tickets to the best concert of the season, Naomi Shemer. Composer-singer Shemer is sort of the Israeli answer to Jacques Brel.

I was trapped. I had no choice. It would be the concert of the season, a real "happening."

We drove to Jerusalem. The concert was brilliant. When she finished, there wasn't a dry eye in the house. After the concert everyone else was too excited just to go home. We went out to eat with some other friends. We didn't get back home until after two. My wife fell into bed exhausted. I peeled off my clothes, took a shower, climbed into bed and stared at the darkness.

The bed felt right. The breeze was delightfully cool. The air was clear and fresh.

I could not sleep. It was the wrong time of the wrong day. Or night. I was no longer tired. I had no idea what time of the day it was for me. Or what day of the week. My biological clock was so out of whack that I couldn't tell if I felt like breakfast or dinner.

At four-thirty the bright sunlight came cascading through the window, and I began to feel tired. By six-thirty, activity began on the Moshav. I could hear voices, cars, men working. I was ready to go to sleep. My kids woke up. They hadn't seen me in days. We all had breakfast together and caught up on each other's activities. It was 9:00 A.M., Neve Ilan time.

I couldn't take it anymore. I fell back into bed. It was time to go to sleep. I put on the radio, so that a soft background of classical music could block out the intermittent irregular sounds of the outside world that might keep me awake.

They were playing the Tchaikovsky violin concerto, with Pearlman. Who else?

I finally fell asleep. A moment later I woke up. I was covered with sweat. It was a warm day, as it often is in August. And the breezes didn't come until evening.

What had awakened me? The music.

Tchaikovsky was over, and it was Beethoven now, not the violin concerto but the Ninth Symphony—the fourth movement, with full chorus singing fortissimo. Not exactly music to sleep by.

I had to turn it off so I could get back to sleep. I wanted to lift up my right arm and reach out and switch off the radio. But I couldn't. My right arm would not move.

I tried again.

My right shoulder—no movement.

My right elbow—no movement.

My right wrist—no movement.

My right hand—no movement.

The fingers of my right hand—no movement.

Perhaps I'd just slept on my right arm wrong and put abnormal pressure on the nerves going into that arm. I hadn't, and I knew it.

Pressure on the nerves always causes sensory problems—not just weakness, but numbness, tingling, and pain.

My arm was not numb. It was not tingling. There was no pain. I knew I was in big trouble.

Another diagnosis posed itself, a far more likely diagnosis: a stroke.

It had to be that; the problem had to be in the brain itself, not in the nerves. I knew that. After all, I was a neurologist.

Total paralysis without sensory loss meant the brain. *A stroke. Damn it all.*

My leg, I thought. Was my right leg also involved? If I'd had a stroke on the left side of my brain, totally paralyzing my right arm, then my right leg should at least be weak, if not equally paralyzed.

I tried to lift it, but I couldn't.

There was no movement of the right hip.

Or the right knee.

Or the right ankle.

Or the right toes.

Nothing—a total wipeout. A total right hemiplegia—a stroke on the left side of my brain.

And the radio kept playing "The Ode to Joy."

Was I aphasic? Even considering the question frightened me, for language was my life.

In almost all right-handed people, the left side of the brain controls speech and language. I was right-handed. I knew I was left-brained. Was my speech affected?

I tried to talk.

No words came out, no words at all.

The simple five-step rule for aphasia that I used to teach medical students leaped into my mind:

1. Aphasia is a loss of the use of language.

2. Aphasia is always due to a lesion of the dominant hemisphere.

3. If the patient has more trouble speaking than understanding, the lesion is toward the front of the left hemisphere.

4. If the patient has more trouble understanding than speaking, the lesion is toward the back of the left hemisphere.

5. And all the rest is mere commentary.

I used this simple program to lead my students through the morass of confusing literature on aphasia. It was simple, accurate, and all they needed to know.

I knew a lot more. I had to—I was a neurologist.

Was my problem one of producing language or understanding it? I listened to Schiller's words. I heard them, and I understood them with no trouble at all.

Thus, the lesion was toward the front. *My* lesion.

It was toward the front of my left hemisphere, just where the motor system started. Just where strokes that caused both hemiplegia and aphasia were located. My problem was not understanding, it was in creating words and language.

But was it? All aphasics have problems in finding the right word. But I could find all the words. I could even translate Schiller's words from German into English, no mean task. No aphasic could do that.

Aphasics have trouble naming objects and remembering names. I could remember names: Beethoven's Ninth.

I thought of the first record of it I'd ever bought: Toscanini, Arturo. That name was too easy, too overlearned. Remembering it proved nothing.

Could I remember the names of the singers on that recording? I could: Farrell, Merriman, Scott, and Pearce. Eileen Farrell. Jan Pearce. Merriman. What was her first name? Lloyd. No. He'd been a reserve outfielder for the Cincinnati Reds.

My memory wasn't perfect. But I was pretty sure I wasn't aphasic, because I could recall names.

Aphasics also have trouble spelling. Could I spell? I was never a great speller anyway.

Toscanini: T-O-S-C-A-N-I-N-I.

And no aphasic could spell backward, but I could: I-N-I-N-A-C-S-O-T.

I was not aphasic. Hemiplegic but not aphasic. But why couldn't I say anything?

Being paralyzed on one-half of the body doesn't make a person mute. It makes the speech slurred; the words that come out sound wrong, but the words do come out. The only way to become unable to make any sounds at all was to be totally paralyzed on both sides. Thus I *had* to be able to say words, or at least syllables. Letters?

I tried again. Toscanini: T-O-S-C-A-N-I-N-I.

I tried to say "T" out loud. Nothing came out. I was mute, wordless, letterless. Mute, not aphasic.

I thus could not have a hemiplegia only.

I tried to move my left arm, but nothing happened.

My left leg—the same lack of results.

So it wasn't hemiplegia; it was double hemiplegia—both sides. Quadriplegia. Total paralysis, including the face and the muscles of speech.

I was saved. I knew that it wasn't a stroke; strokes don't do that. I knew that it was nothing serious at all. I felt like singing.

"The Ode to Joy" was still on the radio. I sang, "Und der Cherub steht vor Gott." And the angels dwell with God.

And as the words burst out of my mouth, my head came off the pillow, my arms jumped into motion, and I was both singing and conducting.

Why not? Toscanini sang as he conducted. If you listen carefully, you can hear his cracked tenor voice on many of his recordings. I sang along to the end. It was not Toscanini; it was Klemperer conducting—with Lovberg, Ludwig, Kmentt, and Hotter.

I turned off the radio, and as I peacefully fell back to sleep, I tried unsuccessfully to recall Merriman's first name.

I had not had a stroke. What I'd had was an episode of sleep paralysis. It used to be rare, but it is no longer quite so rare.

Sleep paralysis was first described as part of the syndrome of narcolepsy, a syndrome the cause of which is unknown. Narcolepsy itself consists of episodic, irresistible attacks of daytime sleepiness. These are not part of normal drowsiness, such as we all have after a big lunch, but sudden episodes of overwhelming sleepiness that cannot be resisted. The attacks often occur when the patient is relaxed or immediately following physical activity. The attacks are sudden and brief. The patient goes to sleep and awakens ten to fifteen minutes later totally refreshed and alert, only to have another such attack later in the day. True narcolepsy is often accompanied by three other types of symptoms, hence the so-called narcoleptic tetrad:

1. Narcolepsy
2. Sleep paralysis
3. Cataplexy
4. Hypnagogic hallucination

Sleep paralysis consists of brief episodes of generalized, but not total, paralysis that occur on awakening from a deep sleep or, more rarely, on falling asleep. The paralysis is not complete. Breathing is not affected, nor is movement of the eyes. I had had no trouble breathing, and I had opened my eyes and been able to move them to see the radio. Also, my paralysis was generalized; the rest of my body was paralyzed and incapable of movement.

The attacks usually last only a minute or two. How long had mine lasted? Seemingly an eternity, but actually no more than two or three variations on the main theme of the fourth movement—four or five minutes at the most.

Attacks of narcolepsy end spontaneously. Those of sleep paralysis are usually interrupted by some external stimulus, a touch or a noise, or by the forceful will of the patient himself. Mine had ended by the joyous singing of Beethoven—a good way to end anything.

Narcolepsy itself is uncommon. It occurs in about one out of a thousand people. Sleep paralysis occurs only in one-quarter of all narcoleptics or one out of four thousand people. Or so we used to think.

Cataplexy consists of attacks of sudden loss of muscle tone. The patient remains conscious, but normal voluntary movement is interrupted. The attacks are fleeting, ending as soon as they have begun. And they are usually brought on by strong emotion—laughter, crying, surprise, anger.

For example, someone is standing at a party, relaxed. Someone else tells a joke—a very good joke. The standing listener laughs heartily. Suddenly he becomes paralyzed and falls to the floor. Then it's over. Once he falls he has no weakness, no paralysis. Nothing is wrong with him. He's embarrassed, but he merely laughed so hard that he fell down. No big deal.

The rarest component of the narcolepsy syndrome is the *hypnagogic hallucinations*. These are generally unpleasant, vivid images that spring into consciousness during periods of drowsiness. Vision, hearing, smell, or all three senses can be involved. These hallucinations occupy the consciousness completely and cannot be resisted; the patient is forced to experience them. They come and go on their own—quickly, spontaneously, irresistibly.

That then is the narcoleptic tetrad. All four components share certain key characteristics: a sudden onset; a spontaneous, irresistible quality that is not under the patient's control; a brief duration; and a sudden return to normal. It's as if someone had turned a switch off and then on—from awake to asleep and back to wakefulness; from movement to no movement to normal movement; from normal thoughts to hallucinations to normal thoughts. And in a way that is what has happened.

Sleep is a process in which the brain remains quite active. The active process of sleep is made up of various stages. Normally, as we enter sleep we slip smoothly from stage to stage like a well-engineered car going from gear to gear as it accelerates or decelerates.

Sleep used to be thought of as a passive process in which the brain rests. It was thought to be passive because what the brain does while asleep is so different from its activities while awake. A number of normal functions of the awake brain have been switched off: muscle tone, muscle movement, conscious thought, and consciousness. And when the person wakes up the next morning, these functions all switch back on.

But what if they don't? What if muscle tone does not switch on when consciousness does? Or if voluntary movement doesn't? What happens is what happened to me: sleep paralysis.

When I awoke, I was totally awake and alert but paralyzed. The neurological gear that shifts from the loss of tone and movement of deep sleep had not become engaged when the one that shifts from deep sleep was somehow jarred into wakefulness.

But, of course, I could breathe, for breathing continues uninterrupted during sleep, so it is immune to this problem. Eye movements also continue during sleep and are therefore spared from sleep paralysis.

Thanks to the age of jet travel, sleep paralysis is no longer rare. A survey of medical students in 1967 revealed that 5 percent had had at least one such episode. My own less scientific survey suggests a much higher incidence. The precipitating factors are like mine: an insult to the biological clock, or abnormal stress to the "gear box" of the brain. Jet lag, fitful abnormal sleep, then sudden awakening with paralysis, often accompanied by anxiety. Always brief. Then back to sleep.

Most people pay no attention to the episodes. Everyone attributes them to jet lag, thinking that it's no big deal.

Most people are not neurologists. They are not worried about hemiplegia and aphasia. They are exhausted travelers who want some sleep and figure it's just jet lag.

The real cause of narcolepsy itself remains unknown, although we understand the physiological aspects. The mechanisms that tie together the brain's various activities no longer work in concert; the gears are stripped. The brain of the jet-lagged traveler returns to normal, and the gears function again, but someone with narcolepsy continues to slip from wakefulness to deep sleep without going through the normal stages in between. He goes from wakefulness to dreaming without sleep and from sleep to wakefulness without muscle tone and has episodes of sudden loss of muscle tone.

About two hours after my brief yet agonizing episode of sleep paralysis, my son woke me up out of my fitful sleep. There was a long-distance phone call for me from the United States. It was the lawyer for whom I had just testified. The case had been decided, and our side had won. "It wasn't so bad, was it?" he asked.

"What?" I replied, still more groggy than awake.

"All the chasing back and forth and the jet lag," he explained. "I'm sure it didn't bother you one bit."

"No," I told him, "not one bit. I never felt better." And in a way I never had. I was as healthy as I had ever been, and having faced the prospect of a significant neurological disease for the first time in my life made me appreciate my good health more than ever before.

17
An Unfulfilled Expectation

Patients and members of their families often have expectations and needs that their physician cannot fulfill. They may make any number of strange requests. This has happened to me more than just occasionally. Some of these requests have been merely unusual or eccentric, while others have been downright outrageous.

I remember a woman named Mrs. Keriazakos who came to see me in 1972. I saw her only once. Not referred by another physician, she had come to me on her own from Iowa. She was a subject at risk for Huntington's chorea. Her mother and her maternal grandfather had died with Huntington's chorea. She had heard that I was interested in predicting which subjects at risk would develop the disease and which ones wouldn't. I could not deny my interest in that question, but that interest was not accompanied by any procedure that had been shown to be reliable. I tried to explain that to her, but she didn't listen to my explanation.

She was forty and looked at least five, perhaps even ten, years younger. Her smile was all but radiant. Aside from her dark hair and eyes, she could have passed for Ingrid Bergman—a Hellenic version of Nordic beauty.

She was also as stubborn as any Hollywood star could possibly be. Test or no test, she needed to know whether she would develop the disease.

Why? I wondered to myself. "You are forty," I said rhetorically.

"You need not remind me."

"You have children."

"Three," she smiled. I loved that smile.

"How old are they?"

"Nineteen, seventeen, and sixteen. The youngest will finish high school next spring. He'll be seventeen then. And I'll be forty-one," she reminded me.

"You don't want to have any more children, do you?"

"Do you think me crazy? That part of my life is over. I can't have any more children. I took care of that a decade ago."

I was at a loss. Normally women and men who were at risk for Huntington's chorea and were without symptoms came to see me with only one question in mind: "If I have children, can I pass this familial taint on to them?" But Mrs. Keriazakos already had her family. If she was destined to get Huntington's chorea and therefore capable of giving it to her children, the harm had already been done.

Perhaps she had symptoms. Perhaps she had noticed something subtle and was worried that she already had Huntington's chorea, and she was challenging me to make the diagnosis. My mother is like that—if the doctor is as good as he's supposed to be, he shouldn't need her to tell him what's wrong.

I went over her neurological and psychiatric history once again, and once again came up empty-handed. So I took her into the examining room. I scrutinized her for all those little things neurologists have reported seeing in Huntington's chorea. I found nothing. The results of her neurological examination were normal.

I went back into my office perplexed. I had no idea why this beautiful woman who had her children and was in perfect health had traveled all the way from Iowa to see me.

She came back into my office and sat down opposite me.

"Mrs. Keriazakos," I began.

"Yvonne," she corrected me.

"Yvonne," I complied. "I do not understand. You are normal now. You have no symptoms. You have your family. You want no other children. What difference would it make if I could tell you you were destined to get Huntington's chorea or not? How could that matter to you? There is nothing we could do to treat you, to prevent the disease from starting if that's going to happen."

"I know that."

"Then how would it change your life?"

"I must know."

Knowledge for the sake of knowledge? I doubted that. "Why?"

"If I am not to get Huntington's chorea, then I will get a divorce as soon as my son graduates from high school, and. . . ." She stopped as if I had no need to know the rest.

"And if not?"

"Then I will stay married to the bastard to whom I am married and let him support me the rest of his life."

There was no real predictive test then. Today chromosomal analysis is about to become available. If it had been available then, would I have arranged for her to get her answer? I suppose so. Patients have the right to have whatever information they need to lead their own lives, and I am in no position to decide their lives for them. But that was 1974. There was really nothing I could do to help her that had proven accuracy. I told her that.

I never saw her again. I have no idea what happened to her or to her marriage or to her children.

My fantasy is that they are all living happily ever after—or at least, if not happily, without Huntington's chorea. That's always my fantasy.

AUTHOR'S NOTE

When I first met Mrs. Keriazakos, I was carrying out studies on the possibility of using various medications to predict the future development of Huntington's chorea in persons at risk for this disorder. It was my interest in this subject that led her to come to see me. Two articles chronicle the use of L-dopa in the presymptomatic detection of Huntington's chorea:

Klawans, H. L., G. W. Paulson, S. P. Ringel, and A. Barbeau. "Use of L-dopa in the detection of presymptomatic Huntington's chorea." *New England Journal of Medicine.* 286: 1332–34 (1972).

Klawans, H. L., C. G. Goetz, S. Pelick. "Presymptomatic and early detection in Huntington's disease." *Annals of Neurology.* 8: 343–47 (1980).

This approach has not proved to be reliable and has now been superseded by recent genetic research. Gene detection in Huntington's chorea is one of the hottest areas in this field. The best recent summary of our scientific knowledge of Huntington's chorea, including the exciting story of locating the gene is:

Martin, J. B., and J. F. Gusella. "Huntington's disease." *New England Journal of Medicine.* 315: 1267–75 (1986).

18

Epilogue: Wanting to Be a Doctor, Part II

Our weakness should make us strong.

In 1986 I published my first short story. It appeared in a now-defunct medical journal called *Medical Heritage*. The story was entitled "Coming Soon to a Book Store Near You." It was about a successful academic physician who wrote a successful novel and about the effect his literary career had on his life in medicine. In it I borrowed one scene from my own life:

It was in November that they made their annual pilgrimage to hear the Boston Symphony String Players give a benefit concert. After the concert was over, they went to a small gathering at the home of some friends. He had been the impressario for the event, she the hostess.

Sam Magid, the first violinist, was there as always. Don recalled another dinner party when they had first met. It must have been six or seven years earlier. Sam had been complaining about the frustrations of his life, sitting in the symphony playing a fiddle day after day. His mother had been right all along. He should have become a physician and helped people. Don had reciprocated and expressed his desire to leave the diseases and tragedies of others behind him, and just once in his life create

something beautiful. Perhaps once, miraculously, for one afternoon, for three hours, they could change places. Sam could run
the cancer clinic and he would become the concert master of the
Boston Symphony. That miracle, of course, had never taken
place. Mark Twain, even fairly good Mark Twain, was out of
style.

Sam did not remember the conversation at all.

The real Sam Magid is Sam Magad, the co-concertmaster of
the Chicago Symphony Orchestra and one of the outstanding
violinists of our time, and he did not remember the conversation at all. The real group was the Chicago Symphony String
Players, and the real conversation took place on a Sunday afternoon about a dozen years ago at a reception for the string
players given by Shom and Herb Klaff. I have retold the story
here only to put my interest in the literary side of my creative
life in proper perspective. I did not always want to be a writer,
but I have wanted to be one for a long time. And now I am one
and, by some standards at least, a fairly successful one. Today
people I meet at cocktail parties all seem to ask me the same
question: "Are you going to give up medicine?" Sometimes
they eliminate any alternative course: "When are you going to
give up medicine?"

The answer should be obvious, even to the most casual observer. I will not give up the practice of medicine to become a
full-time writer. I understand now far better than I did when I
applied to medical school just why I want to be a doctor. It's not
because I want to learn more about the nervous system and
how it works. It's not to teach or to do research. Those pursuits
have some importance, but they are not the reason I have no
interest in changing my job description. The fact is that all of
the clichés I heard from my father had more than just an
element of truth in them. Taking care of sick people, inserting
your life and skills into their lives, and allowing their lives and
problems and tragedies into your life is the best way I know to
live life to its fullest. No matter what good I have done for my
patients, they have done more for me. They have taught me as
much as I have ever taught any medical student and about far
more than the brain and the spinal cord.

One of my patients wrote a brief article for a Spanish lay organization of patients with Parkinson's disease. It was his manifesto for his fellow patients. He recited it to me during one of his visits to Chicago:

> Our weakness should make us strong.
> Our rigidity should make us flexible.
> Our tremors should give firmness to our resolve.
> Our depression should clarify our thoughts.
> We must not accept deterioration with resignation, but with the pride that comes from winning the battle that we fight each and every day of our lives.

I cannot stop doing my best to assist such patients in their daily struggles to make their lives better.

About the Author

Dr. Harold L. Klawans is professor of neurology and pharmacology at Rush University in Chicago, editor in chief of the journal *Clinical Neuropharmacology,* an editor of *The Handbook of Clinical Neurology,* and the author of more than three hundred scientific articles and three novels.